MW00931237

SIBLING LOSS

A Sister's Journey from Despair to Celebration

.

Laura Prince

Copyright © 2017 Laura Prince
All rights reserved.

ISBN: 1539389375
ISBN 13: 9781539389378

PRAISE FOR *SIBLING LOSS*

"Laura Prince offers us a painful, yet enlightening, glimpse into the distorted world that becomes home to a child who has lost a sibling. Her pain flows through the pages in ways I believe she may not even be aware. It is in the retelling of her quest for the unconditional love only her lost brother could give her that the pain becomes excruciating to the reader.

Laura Prince has 'broken the silence.' She has written a book that is, unfortunately, quite unique. Perhaps the grip sibling death has on the survivors' lives reaches so far into the future, few have ever been able to extricate themselves from the suffocating web to share the grief and verbalize the unspeakable. Children grieve in the same way they laugh and love – in a manner which is uncontrollable, unconditional, and often unending."

Judith Kovalski, M.A., M.S.W.,
Hope & Cope, Sir Mortimer B. Davis – Jewish General Hospital

"*Sibling Loss* by Laura Prince is an impassioned, heartfelt, personal account of the death of her young brother. Each word and thought strikes a chord in the life of even those who have not lost a sibling because it validates the feelings and fears associated with various losses people experience in their lifetimes. For those who have lost a sibling or a parent, or are in a relationship with someone who has,

Prince reveals the lifelong process of healing. For those in the helping professions, Prince awakens us to the needs of those who are grieving and to ways of helping both individuals and families break their silence, and maintain an awareness of one another and sense of intimacy. Prince helps us to realize that love of another person transcends all space and time and shapes our lives long after the event of physical death."

Deborah Witt Sherman, Ph.D., R.N.,
Assistant Professor, Division of Nursing, New York University

"*Sibling Loss* by Laura Prince is the best story illustrating the long-term consequences of unresolved childhood grief that I have seen. As a culture, we believe either that children do not grieve, or that they get over their grief more quickly than do adults. Nothing could be further from the truth. Laura Prince tells her family's story simply, and therefore beautifully and effectively. This book will be a treasure both for those who are grieving and for those working with the grieving."

John D. Morgan, Ph.D.,
*Coordinator, King's College Centre for Education
about Death and Bereavement*

"This book is no slouch when it comes to insight, to thought provoking and emotionally stirring observations and sharing. It is tough reading and it is *honest* reading. It is a book that will keep you spellbound, for you really are reading a person's diary through grief, but you will be frequently distracted. I found myself marking the margins on almost every page with her brilliant insights and trusting vulnerability, and from her sharing, wrote what seemed like volumes of marginal notes because thoughts and feelings were penetrated within me.

The book (and all names are fictitious) is the diary of a woman bereaved, and how the dynamics of misguided grief, strong family values often expressed in denial and conflict, and the long term effects of mourning denied, and thus become complicated, that the author experienced. We see the strong values of culture as a compromiser, the differences afforded expressions of grief because of the nature of the relationship or the age/generation of the mourner, expressions of sorrow rooted in the inability to find a meaningful relationship, sexual wanderings in hopes of "curing" the pain, and, in many ways, one of the most graphic expressions of the real challenges of sibling loss as they emerge in the child and often do not find expression and relief until well into adult life.

The book is dedicated to the memory of "Mathew," and it is the story of the author's having to come to terms (grieve!) with the death of her brother."

The Rev. Fr. Richard B. Gilbert,
Executive Director, The World Pastoral Care Center

This book was written in loving memory of my brother Mathew (1949-1963)
It is dedicated to my brothers Steven and Marc, and to all other children of
families who have experienced the tragedy of the loss of a sibling.
Although this book is an actual family account, it is based on my own memo-
ries and perceptions. The names and places have been changed to protect the
privacy of my family.

http://siblinglossblog.com

TABLE OF CONTENTS

PREFACE

In his book *Changer La Mort*, the renowned French palliative physician Dr. Leon Schwartzenberg refers to a comment made by a mother whose twenty-year-old son is dying. Translated into English, the essence of her comment is that in every language there is a word for someone who has lost a father; one is an orphan. If one has lost a husband, one is a widow. However, there is no word in any language for someone who has lost a child, so unnatural is this happening. In effect, what this mother is saying is that the death of a child is so traumatic and so painful that no one in any country has been able to come up with the words to identify the surviving members of the family.

When someone you love moves away from you, regardless of the distance that separates you, you are comforted by the possibility of reunion. But when someone you love dies, the hope for reunion is gone. Twenty seven years ago, my thirteen-year-old brother Mathew was accidentally killed by a car while riding his bicycle to a baseball game. My family became, and has remained, completely silent regarding this tragedy. We never worked out the anguish of it together or with close friends or clergy. At that time, society was not as well equipped with grief-therapy treatment as it is today. Because my parents' loss was so devastating, my brothers' and my loss became secondary to them, and therefore our grief was never resolved.

When my brother Mathew was killed, I was sixteen, my brother Steven was twenty, and my brother Marc was almost twelve. Although our family had many problems before my brother's death, as most families have, this greatly amplified our dysfunction as a family unit, for unknown to us, he was our underlying stabilizer. After his death, and the ensuing silence, my brothers and I developed a negative and destructive manner towards one another. Mathew's demise left an irreversible void, an emptiness that could never be filled by anyone else. However, that emptiness could have been somewhat alleviated by a heartfelt exchange in dialogue, but my family was incapable of this method of release.

This book is my attempt at freeing myself by breaking our silence. I hope my story will encourage you to break your silence, as well.

1

WILL

When I was about nineteen, I met a boy, Will, on a weekend outing to the Laurentians, who had been introduced by a mutual friend. After that weekend, Will and I became steady partners for the next couple of years. I viewed Will as not only a distraction from my boredom and loneliness, but also as a possible escape from what I had come to believe was an unhappy and imprisoned existence at home. Somehow I had formed the idea that I could never leave home and take care of myself, so I needed someone to help me get away. Although Will was wild, undisciplined, and very spoiled, I convinced myself that I loved him.

When I was in my third year of university, Will asked me to marry him and I jumped at the chance. This also gave my family an opportunity to indulge in some party-making on my behalf, which I felt would help them take their minds off my brother Mathew's death. We announced our engagement during the winter of my last year at university, and then made all the arrangements for a huge wedding. This kept both families busy for months.

I finished my studies at Sir George in May of 1968; then I wrote my exams during the month of June amidst all the excitement of my wedding plans. The wedding itself turned out to be a huge success. However, the morning of the wedding, as we were preparing to leave the house for the synagogue, Dad passed out in the foyer.

He didn't seem to be breathing. Mom remembered that we had a neighbour down the street who was a doctor, and sent Marc running down our block to try and reach him. Thank goodness he was home and came over immediately. Mom explained as quickly as she could about the medications Dad was taking for his depression and his diabetes. The doctor administered a shot and then resuscitated my father. When dad regained consciousness, he said he was well enough to go out, so we carefully maneuvered him into the car and drove to the synagogue. Once there, we placed Dad in a chair while we all prepared ourselves for the photo session. Proof of Dad's dazed condition remains, to this day, in the photos. Everything continued as planned, but we were all completely unnerved by this experience. I know that if I had been a bit older, and the synagogue hadn't been so full of activity, I would have cancelled the whole ceremony. Although I finally did enjoy myself, I was angry about the size of the affair, as I only knew about half the people who were invited. I also felt that my parents had spent far too much money, and that the wedding was done as much for show as it was done for the two of us.

Will and I spent ten days of our honeymoon at the Calgary Stampede in Alberta. Even though there were some wonderful moments, I was appalled at how extravagant Will was with our wedding gift money. I was even more worried that most of the time we were there I wished that I wasn't with him. When we returned from Alberta, we went to Freeport in the Bahamas for a week. While I sunbathed, all Will did was gamble in the hotel casino. We returned to Montreal considerably poorer, which further distressed me. Then real married life began after we drove to Toronto to live in the apartment we reserved a few months earlier.

My graduation was supposed to be the next big event in my family's life. I was to be the first female in the Roth-Steiner clan with a university degree. However, when I received my marks, I found out that I failed my course in Law, the one course that wasn't required for my major, and that I would have to write a supplemental exam during the summer, which, of course, cancelled my graduation plans with my fellow school-mates.

I was literally crestfallen by this failure. I also couldn't pass the supplemental exam. Will wasn't bothered by this, as he felt that a young woman had no need for a higher education, so he was no support to me at all. My brother Marc, on the other hand, expressed how badly he felt for me. My other brother, Steven, who had also failed his last year in university, didn't have any comment, probably because he couldn't believe that something like this could happen twice in the same family. It was my parents' total lack of sympathy and undisguised disappointment that really hit me the hardest. I hated them because of their attitude, and never really forgave them.

When Will and I moved to Toronto, I still needed one course to complete my Bachelor of Arts degree in Psychology. Once there, I inquired at Simon Fraser University about taking a make-up course. The admissions officer was very receptive, but informed me that I would have to acquire a degree from their university, even though I had passed ninety-nine percent of my program somewhere else. I refused to comply with this regulation, convincing myself that I would somehow obtain my degree in the future at Sir George. I had no idea what I wanted to do as far as a career was concerned, and it didn't matter. What did matter was that I had succeeded in getting away from home, and after having seen my family's reaction to my not graduating, my need for escape became even stronger.

I finally had true anonymity with Will in Toronto. Although he proved to be completely wrong for me, just having the opportunity to arrange my own home and live in another environment was my very first step towards personal freedom. While I busied myself decorating my new apartment, the shackles of home and the sad memories I had there seemed distant.

We drove to Montreal to see our respective families about once a month, and I soon realized how important these trips were for me because I got a dose of love from my family each time we visited. Love was the missing ingredient in my marriage. Will wanted little more than a constantly available sexual partner, as well as a showpiece for his friends and associates to admire and envy.

Living with Will was like an emotional and intellectual rape. His father worked for the largest receivership company in Montreal. Even before we were married, I made myself party to criminal activities by agreeing, on a couple of occasions, to accompany them during the evening to bankrupt stores and helping myself, with their encouragement, to whatever I wanted. They assured me that what we were doing was perfectly legal and wouldn't affect the store owners' bankruptcy status. I only went on two of these expeditions, for I thought they were shady and told Will that if he continued to participate in them with his father, I wouldn't marry him. However, nothing could change the background that Will had been raised in. He was coarse, possessive, lazy, and dishonest to the core. Within months of our wedding, we began to fight viciously with one another.

During our first year of marriage, I had an affair with a wild and exciting colleague, whom I worked with in real-estate, and cherished every moment we spent together. Caro was about twelve years older than me. Although in the beginning he was only interested in me sexually, I didn't care because he was so much fun to be with.

Because Caro was compassionate and very tender, he was also the first stranger who I ever spoke to at length about my family's tragedy. I remember how he rocked me in his arms while I wept, and how, to my astonishment, he wept with me. No one had reached out to alleviate my pain since I had told my friend Josie about Mathew's death and how it affected me. Even though this happened only once, I felt a tremendous sense of release from this experience. Will never wanted me to discuss Mathew's death, for he admitted that it frightened him to see me in a state of despair.

Even though I was terrified that Will might find out what I was up to, I continued my clandestine affair. One evening, when Will was supposed to be out of town on a business trip, I went over to visit Caro. I came home very late only to find Will waiting for me in the apartment. He told me that he suspected that I was seeing someone else, and that if it was true he would kill the guy and make life miserable for me. I retorted that his suspicions were insane and that I was already miserable living with him. He changed jobs three times during the first year we were married; had seemed to need every cent I made; had bought things we couldn't possibly afford, which I had to force him to return; and, in general, had criticized me and my family constantly.

I concealed my problems with Will from my family, not only because I was ashamed, but also because I was used to their general lack of support and I was afraid of their reactions to my failure at marriage. Besides this, they spent so much money on our wedding and it had been only a year since I failed to graduate. Even though I knew they didn't like Will, I still couldn't confide in them about how helpless and unhappy I felt.

Eventually, however, the situation between Will and I became unbearable enough for me to end our marriage. During our second year together, I discovered that Will and three of his friends had been charged with "gross indecency" by one of the young girls who worked in his office. His father managed to pull some legal strings and the charges were dropped, but after that incident I hardly ever slept with Will again. Often, in the middle of the night, I would get out of bed and go down the hall to the living-room to sleep beside our dog Dutch; then just before it was time to get up in the morning, I would creep back into our bed and pretend that I had been there all night. It was on these nights that I often contemplated suicide.

One afternoon I came home from work to find Will in the apartment, standing in the middle of a mountain of rubble, paper, and clothes. He explained that he desperately needed to repay a debt he owed to some dangerous people – people who were threatening him with bodily harm – so he had feigned a robbery for the purpose of collecting insurance money.

I started to rave uncontrollably, asking him why he told me about the "perpetration" at all, instead of just letting me think that our place had been vandalized and robbed. He cruelly replied that he wanted to make sure I was implicated enough so that I would never be able to report him. Furthermore, he informed me that he had already called the police, who would be arriving momentarily. He then proceeded to show me a list of things which we were to confirm had been stolen from the apartment, including our stereo equipment and all of my jewellery. It was at that instant that I became utterly terrified of Will, for I could see how demented he really was. I stood there in complete shock and horror while he told me where he had hidden all of these "stolen things" that we were about to swear had been taken from our place. He tried to console me by assuring me that he would have all the jewellery reset sometime in the future, so that it could never be traced. I began to laugh and told him that I thought this was a pretty poor joke and that he should own up to the farce, but, to my horror, he calmly told me that it was all true.

When the police arrived, I reluctantly went through the exercise that Will had so skillfully prepared for me. After they filled out a report and left, I became completely disgusted with what I had been party to. I was also in a state of rage and hated Will for having done this to me. I made him promise that my signature would not be required for the insurance claim because I definitely wouldn't sign it. Will, with his criminal and obviously deranged mind, believed me. I pretended that everything would be alright as long as we never spoke of the incident again.

The next morning, I called in sick in order to fix up the apartment. I encouraged Will to go to work and said that I would take care of the clean-up. As soon as I was sure he was gone, I packed a suitcase, took all of my jewellery from its hiding place, then called my Uncle Ezra and Aunt Rhonda to come and pick me up. I told them that I was leaving Will and that I needed a place to stay for a couple of days until my parents could come and pick me up.

During the first day I was at my uncle and aunt's home, I had to go settle things at work and close my bank account. I called a cab and told the driver to take a long ride, occasionally asking him to stop and let me out for a few moments. In a period of an hour, I threw all of my jewellery down the sewers of Toronto, as having it in my possession was literally making me ill.

When I returned to my relative's home, I called Will at the apartment to advise him that I had left him. I also told him that I would be fetching my things within a few days and that he was to make sure he wasn't there when I came to collect them. After he was reasonably convinced that I meant what I said, Will informed me that he couldn't find the jewellery and asked me where it was. When I explained to him that I had no idea, he was furious. He actually wanted some of it for himself, despite the fact that he was collecting the insurance! He also insinuated that I had hidden it away somewhere. I held my ground and insisted that I had no idea where it was, and that, if he ever found it, I wanted no part of it.

My parents arrived in Toronto a few days later to help me move my things back home. Of course I hadn't been able to tell them anything regarding the real reasons why I had left Will; consequently, they were a bit alarmed at my condition, for I was upset and frightened to a degree that they found exaggerated. However, because they disliked Will intensely, they were noticeably relieved that I would no longer be living with him, and, strangely enough, I could also see that they wanted me home again.

Due to the shock treatments and the medication, Dad snapped out of his depression one day just as fast as he had fallen into it. That was about a year after Will and I were married. Just prior to this change Marc was just leaving home, and I was already having serious problems with Will. I'm sure that my father blamed the incident of his depression as being the major contributing factor in my going ahead with a marriage he didn't agree with, as well as his son moving out at such a young age, otherwise he would have done his best to prevent both.

My parents helped me through the shock of both my separation and my divorce. For the first time in years, I really felt that they came through for me. I moved back into their house, not only angry and depressed, but also penniless. My marriage to Will had galled me to a degree that I wanted nothing that had been connected to my association with him. I took only my personal belongings and the wedding gifts I received from my close friends and relatives, and left everything else behind. Because Will didn't believe I would honour this gesture of contempt that he stupidly interpreted as either insanity or generosity on my part, he was overjoyed when I suggested that I would leave him all of our belongings on the condition that he would give me a divorce, which he agreed to. I was thrilled to be rid of him, for he is one of the few people in my past that I still regret having known and having wasted my time with.

2

MY FAMILY BACKGROUND AND HOW MY PARENTS MET

So how exactly did I get into this complicated web of grief, and regret? As in all stories, there is a beginning that takes us step by step to the present time. My story began long ago, with those of my parents.

My mother's parents were both born and raised in Russia. They met when they were in their early twenties and were married in Odessa. My maternal grandfather, who owned a shoe factory, became a successful businessman, and his family enjoyed an affluent lifestyle for many years. Together they had five children, all boys, except for my mother who was the youngest child. The age difference between my mother and her brothers was two, five, seven, and twelve years.

In 1922, due to the political pressure from the Communists and the mounting prejudice against Jews, one night in secret the family fled Russia for Poland. They left behind their beautiful home, their business, their friends everything for what was to be the beginning of a long journey across Europe. That journey would eventually lead them to America.

My mother's family remained in Poland for over three years, until political and social pressures once again grew dangerous enough for them to leave. They fled in secret, then proceeded across Europe by train and car until they reached Paris. They chose France because, besides being the farthest country they could travel to, it was also the —easiest place from which to reach America. America was their final, planned destination, where they hoped to start a new life.

It took a while for my mother's family to get settled in Paris. The boys spoke a little French, which they had learned in school, but as they were Russian refugees, they still had difficulty integrating into a new society. In case the family's stay was to be long-term, my maternal grandparents rented an affordable room in a small building in Argenteuil, a suburb way out of the city. My Uncle Miron, who was the eldest son, was sent to board with a family in Paris so that he could enroll in a university and continue his studies in dentistry, which he'd already begun in Poland. He still came home on weekends to visit his family.

During the time that the family was adjusting themselves to their new life in Argenteuil, my grandfather wrote to his brother who had left Russia many years before and was now living in New York. His brother wrote back and told my grandfather that he should immigrate to New York, as there were employment opportunities for him. However, it took several months for my grandfather to get all the necessary papers in order to finally secure passage by ship to the United States.

Unfortunately, when he arrived in New York City, his brother met him with the disappointing news that the situation had changed and there was no work available at that time for him. My grandfather was then rerouted to Montreal. In Montreal, through the help network for Russian refugees, he secured shelter and, eventually, a job. This unexpected change of plans being in a strange country with no family or friends at all was a terrible shock to him and left him completely alone for the first time in his life.

Before he set sail for America, my grandfather had organized everything for his family's security. He had settled them in Argenteuil and had made sure they had all the necessary documents to guarantee that their stay in France would continue without complications.

Miron's boarding arrangements and university program had been finalized, and my mother and her other brothers had all been enrolled in schools. He also secured part-time jobs for the three eldest boys at a train-station loading dock, where they worked after school and on weekends in order to save money.

After my grandfather left, my grandmother, the boys, and my mother all continued to live in their one small room, which was about fifteen-feet square. There was no running water and no refrigerator. A heating element with only one burner served as a stove. They had to pump their water from an outside well that was about seventy-five feet from their building. A hole in the floor of an outhouse, which served as their toilet, was across the back courtyard.

They shopped daily for their food, and my grandmother somehow managed to cook meals one pot full at a time on her one burner. There was a table in the room that served as both an eating place and also as a desk to do homework on. There were two double beds in the room, one of which was right up against the table so that two people could sleep in it without anyone falling off. My grandmother and mother shared that bed, and the three brothers slept together in the other bed. While my grandfather still lived there, two of the boys slept on the floor, and the three youngest shared one bed. However, despite their hardships, during the years that they lived in this crowded room, my mother recalls my grandmother often saying that although they spent them in relative poverty compared to the luxury they had been used to in Russia, they were among the happiest she had ever known. She remembered a dreadful insecurity and fear accompanying that luxury, even before the Communists took over. Here, she was safe with all her children around her, in this tiny but womb-like abode.

When her family first arrived in Paris, my mother was seven and her brother Mathew was almost ten. Miron was nineteen, Soula was seventeen, and Siah was fifteen. The three eldest children were almost always away from the house, either at school or at work. Unfortunately, because they had no father to guide them during these impressionable years, they went a bit astray. Siah started gambling a little, and Soula was running around with older women. Only Miron was proud and stern. Because he was the oldest, he felt responsible for his two younger brothers, but, due to a heavy study schedule, he had no time to scrutinize their behaviour. He concentrated more on being a father-figure to my mother and his youngest brother Mathew. Miron always tried to provide comfort and hope for his mother in order to help her through the trauma of being separated from her husband.

My mother adored her brother Mathew. He had an even temperament and was gentle, kind, and patient; Mathew wasn't complicated with vanities like her other brothers were. Due to being so close in age, Mathew and my mother were constantly together, and nurtured one another throughout their travels. As a result, they provided the necessary friendship and moral support that they each desperately needed while going through every terrifying change of country, language, and culture.

After having spent three years in Montreal, my grandfather had thoroughly established himself. He found a good job in a shoe factory, which enabled him to save quite a bit of money, so he secured jobs for his two middle sons and sent for them. However, my Uncle Miron, who had finished dentistry by this time, was seeing a French woman that he was planning to marry, and therefore chose to remain in France. Consequently, my grandmother, who had become used to having her brood around her, suddenly found herself with only her two youngest children. The three of them spent one more year in Argenteuil waiting to be reunited with the rest of the family. When they were finally able to leave, my mother was thirteen years old and her brother Mathew was fifteen.

It was 1932 when my grandmother, my mother, and her brother arrived in Montreal. My grandmother had now been separated from my grandfather for over five years and, although it must have been wonderful for them to be back together again, it must have also been difficult as so many changes had taken place. In the same way, even though it must have been a joy for my mother and her brother Mathew to be reunited with their father, leaving France had severed them from the only place they ever considered as home and everything they remembered as being safe. Now they had to start all over again, and despite the fact that everyone assured them that this move would be their last, my mother and Mathew recalled all the fears they had seen in the other family members' faces at the time of those other beginnings. Nevertheless, they were thankful to have the familiarity of one another, as everyone else felt somewhat out of touch. My grandfather, however, never really got to know his two youngest children again because he died within five years of their arrival, due to the strain of his turbulent life. His legacy to his family was the slipper factory, which he had come to own, and they continued to work there as a team for many years.

By the time they were all reunited, my mother's family had overcome almost insurmountable obstacles. The trauma and terror of those experiences were permanently etched into their lives. Although they had one another to rely on and trust over the years, they had obviously not been able to trust outsiders. Those first two secretive and dangerous moves left them wary of strangers, for they had learned that anonymity was a necessary attribute of survival. Because of this, my mother's family forever kept silent about the true nature of their experiences even to us. They spoke only of their final success and not about the enormous emotional investment that it had taken to achieve that success.

My father's parents were also born and raised in Russia. My paternal grandmother came from the large city of Rostov and my grandfather originated from Kalarache, a small village. They immigrated to Canada at the turn of the century when they were in their mid-twenties and eventually met in Montreal, where, only a few years later, they were married. However, unlike my mother's parents, they had both come voluntarily to build a new life in a free country. Although my paternal grandfather occasionally exhibited a dry sense of humour, he was generally a quiet and serious man who had bouts of anger and depression. My father's mother, on the other hand, was a lively and cheerful, but overbearing woman. A true matriarch, she assumed complete control of the raising of her three sons.

My father's parents ran a small grocery store from a converted section of their flat. They struggled like most immigrant families trying to make ends meet, but because they had no relations in Canada to depend on for help, their situation was all the more difficult. However, despite their initial hardships, my grandfather eventually found a job as an upholsterer in a factory, which had been his original trade. As a result of working too many hours, he became quieter and surlier with age; and his lack of relaxation time deprived him of any of life's pleasures, especially the joy of getting to know his own sons. Because he became progressively more introverted as he got older, I remember perceiving him as a depressed man who was fed up with his environment.

On the other hand, my grandmother's self-denial of worldly and material pleasures left her with her sons as her only source of happiness, a situation that was unfortunately typical of families in those days. Due to the fact that my grandfather expressed little affection for, or approval of, his sons, my father and his brothers were overly attached to their mother. She became their major source of love and they always had her full attention.

Of their three sons, my father was the eldest. Henry was the middle boy, three years younger than Dad, and Ely was the youngest, born six years after Henry. The three boys were very attached to one another, and although they each made their own friends, they maintained a special closeness. Because Ely was the baby, his mother and brothers pampered him. However, as the years passed, the gap in age difference widened between Ely and his two older brothers. Henry and Dad became even closer, but Ely was somewhat left out of the original threesome.

When he was only thirteen, my father had to leave school to help support the family. It was the beginning of the Depression and my grandparents couldn't make ends meet by their efforts alone, so my father went to work in his parents' grocery store in order to save them the expense of hiring an employee. Although he had all the standard pressures that first-born children usually have to bear, he was robbed of his youth by having to go to work at such a young age.

My father managed to finish high school by attending night classes, and I've always admired the spirit and tremendous effort this must have taken. His brother Henry was only able to complete up to grade eight, then he also had to go and work with my father and my grandmother in the grocery store. Having his brother with him during the day gave my father the much needed youthful company he had to give up when he left school. Before this, while he had worked alone with my grandmother in the store, my father had waited anxiously for Henry to come home from classes so that they could deliver beer and groceries together. During these afternoons, they horsed around by pulling one another all over the Park Avenue area in a small wagon that had been a favourite childhood toy, and this had provided daily comic relief for both of them.

Ely was able to finish high school, and through the financial support of his two older brothers, was enrolled in university to fulfil his wish of becoming a doctor. However, neither my father nor his brother, Henry, ever felt that Ely appreciated the sacrifice they had made for him, because Ely never mentioned it later in life. Because he hadn't experienced the hardship of working as a youth, Ely didn't understand the extent of their sacrifice at the time. It never occurred to him that the money they gave for his education might have made a great deal of difference to his brothers' futures, which was especially true in my father's case.

A couple of years after my father stopped attending school during the day, his uncle offered him employment in one of his jewellery stores. Because his uncle was the only successful and independent business man in the family, my grandmother encouraged my father to accept this offer - my father also saw this opportunity as a big step upward. Unfortunately, no one in the family knew that his uncle was an extremely critical man who was dreadful to work for, and, right from the beginning, he treated my father in the most horrid manner.

The respect that my father received from his family for securing this job was little reward for the daily stress he bore. Even though his son's self-esteem and confidence were progressively being destroyed by this monstrous man, my grandfather did nothing about Dad's problems with his uncle. Like most simple, hard working men who never acknowledge their own worth, my grandfather only saw that his brother-in-law was rich and greatly admired by my grandmother. Therefore, he felt his brother-in-law was justified in whatever he was doing while employing his son. Also, because my grandfather and my father hardly communicated, my father was unable to express the gravity of his situation. He was trapped, and no one came to his rescue.

My father's uncle criticized him constantly and never appreciated his efforts, even though all his efforts always paid off, for what better victim could he have had than a boy whose help was mandatory for the mainstay of his family? His uncle knew that my father couldn't complain openly as everyone was depending on him. Because my father persevered, everyone expected him to become a prodigious businessman, but they didn't realize how little instruction and encouragement he was being given. Since he was afraid of disappointing everyone, that fear compounded his anger over what he felt was an unsolvable situation. My father was never shown the compassion he so desperately needed in order to survive those difficult years; consequently, he never had much sympathy for anyone else after that. It was only after he met my mother that there was any relief from all the anger he had collected and suppressed, for she was the one person who supported him completely and loved him, no matter what.

My father had already been working in one of his uncle's jewellery stores for about four years when, by chance, my mother walked in to buy a watch for her boyfriend's birthday. Later, when we were grown up, my father told us that while he made the sale to my mother, he became "utterly smitten" with her. He quickly devised some flaw in the watch she had chosen, told her that he would fix it, and then deliver it to her home that same evening, so she gave him her address.

It turned out that he didn't have to travel very far, as my mother only lived a couple of blocks from his home. To this day, it's always amazed me that they never met before this during the five years that they lived almost next door to one another. The day after he delivered the watch to her home, my mother realized that she, too, was very attracted to my father. She promptly dropped her boyfriend and immediately after, my parents' love affair began.

My mother represented the realization of my father's every desire. She was not only strong-willed and confident, but also a classical blonde beauty with a sexual allure and a sense of humour that any man would find irresistible. For example, she once told us of an amusing incident that had happened before she met Dad. She was driving downtown in her car when she caught sight of a really good looking man, and was so distracted by him, that she drove on to the sidewalk and into a pole!

My father was also the fulfillment of my mother's dreams. He was a handsome, young, athletic type who displayed every promising feature of success. He was also a truly sensitive, romantic, and loving man. For instance, he often brought Mom and her mother flowers and small gifts.

My parents would frequently take long walks together, and because he was so entranced by her, he occasionally bumped into things. On one of those walks, he couldn't take his eyes off her and subsequently fell off the sidewalk and landed flat on his face. Another time, to demonstrate his strength, he carried her up three flights of stairs to her front door. Their relationship was filled with laughter, and I relished every detail they ever told me about this stage of their lives, for it illustrated how fresh and innocent their beginning had been.

My parents were married in 1939, just eighteen months after they had met. My mother was twenty and my father was twenty-one years old, and, although my maternal grandfather died before this union, my maternal grandmother accepted my father into her family with great joy.

Because my parents' families lived in close-walking distance, it was easy for the two grandmothers to get to know one another, and, to the delight of all their children, they developed a wonderful friendship. However, ever since the time of her arrival in Montreal, my mother had grown progressively more and more distant from her brothers Siah and Soula. The reason for this was that she felt that the moral structure of her two brothers had deteriorated. Siah had become a gambler and Soula had become a playboy. My mother and Soula also had a disagreement over the family business and, as a result of this, coupled with her adverse feelings about his lifestyle, they stopped speaking to one another. Therefore, my father and his brother Henry only had the opportunity to get close to their brother-in-law, Mathew, whom they became very fond of.

Although my parents were fortunate because they were married at the end of the Depression, just as the world started to benefit from a better economy, the Second World War was declared. It was 1943 when our families first became affected. My mother's brother, Mathew, was called in to train for the air corps while my father's brother, Henry, was drafted into the army. My father was conscripted into the air corps, but, thankfully, he served in Canada. The year that my father was drafted, my brother Steven was born. Two years later, in 1945, and only months before the war ended, Mathew and Henry were sent overseas to England to fight.

3

OUR EARLY YEARS

During the three years that my father served in the air corps, my mother completely immersed herself in her maternal role. She therefore had the time to establish a powerful bond with Steven, just as her mother had done twenty years earlier with her own children. However, due to his absence, my father's bond with Steven was never really established in those formative years.

Of my two uncles who had been sent overseas in 1945, Henry was the lucky one - he returned. My Uncle Mathew did not. The War Office informed my mother's family that he had been shot down with his squadron only weeks before the war ended. None of his fellow officers could find him after their plane crashed, so he was reported as missing. Although, by the end of that year he was presumed dead, it hadn't been confirmed, and a two-year period of silent hope and terror passed for my family. In 1947, they received the horrifying news that his dog tags had been found in Germany. A few months later, because she couldn't live with the reality of her son's death, my maternal grandmother died. My mother had now lost two of the most important people in her life within the same year, and, as a result, a major part of her life-long support system was gone. Although I have never been able to discuss this with my mother, I believe that the confirmation of her brother's death almost destroyed her emotionally. And I also believe that because my maternal grandmother was so consumed by her own grief, she was unable to render any comfort for her daughter in order to help her cope with the loss of her brother.

I was born shortly before my family learned of my Uncle Mathew's death. Steven was already four years old, and, although he and I needed her and could have provided a superb distraction for her grief, something happened to my mother that year that left its mark on us. Mathew had been her most cherished life-long friend, and I believe her anguish over his death affected everyone around her.

Because Steven and my mother had developed such a close bond, he reacted to my mother's sorrow in two ways; he felt responsible for her happiness, but, on the other hand, he also felt abandoned. My father was unable to provide Steven with the attention that he lacked from my mother, as he was struggling for her attention himself. The nurse, whom my mother had hired to help her, didn't improve matters or the way Steven felt. Therefore, Steven became particularly attentive towards me, and he and I found in each other the love that my mother was unable to give us at that time.

Like all newborn babies, I was up every couple of hours for the first few months, but, eventually, I began to sleep through the night. Steven, on the other hand, had been a particularly bad sleeper and a poor eater from the time that he was born. My parents put me in the same room with him to see if having some company would help him sleep better, which it did. We shared a room for a couple of years, and Steven finally slept in peace.

During this period, Steven and I became inseparable friends, and his affection towards me eventually overrode his initial resentment. Although he was no longer the center of attention, having someone who was there just for him--to teach, direct, and play with--made up for it. We were wonderful playmates together.

After those first few years, I lost Steven's ever-present company when he started school. He made new friendships there, and, although it hurt me, I enjoyed having my mother to myself for the first time in my life. However, this only lasted for a short period because she was six-months pregnant and due to have a baby in December.

I was two years and ten-months old when my brother Mathew was born. My parents named him in memory of my Uncle Mathew. I took advantage of my chance to get close to my mother again by throwing myself into the almost instinctive role of "little mother." I could now take care of someone as my brother Steven had done with me. I loved Mathew selflessly right from the beginning, and received him into my life like some sort of heavenly gift. I was completely captivated by him; he was such a good-natured and funny baby. Besides his having such an exquisite face, I was also fascinated by the expression of peace in his eyes, which no one else in the family had. Even when I was a little girl, Mathew's eyes somehow soothed me, for when I gazed into them, all my fears vanished.

Steven was also taken with Mathew. Although he and I were still close, Steven was gone a large part of the day which gave me lots of time to spend with Mathew, and less and less time to spend with him. As a result, Steven and I began to drift apart, and that must have been very difficult for him because he had never had to share me with anyone before.

When Mathew was born, the apartment in the Park Avenue area became too small for all of us to live in. My parents had rented it seven years earlier when they were first married. As there were only two bedrooms in the flat, the one that Steven and I had shared now became Mathew's and my sleep quarters at night, as well as a room for all three of us to play in during the day. Steven slept in the living-room on the couch. This arrangement didn't last very long as my parents immediately began to look for a larger place to live.

Within months of Mathew's birth, my family moved out of the apartment and into a beautiful, large, upper-duplex in Outremont. Mathew and I continued to share a bedroom, and Steven now had a room of his own. The street we lived on was lined with magnificent old maple trees, and Steven, Mathew, and I were enchanted by the squirrels and birds that we could see close up from our balcony. Every day, milk was delivered to our door by a horse-drawn wagon. I loved seeing the wagon come and go, and I even liked the smell of the horse manure that was left on our block. It was only a one-minute walk down the road to a large street called Van Horne, which we loved because the store windows were filled with delicious things to eat and a colourful array of wondrous things to look at.

My parents allowed Steven and me to play outside either on the sidewalk in front of our house, or on our balcony, which was fenced-up high above our heads by a strong meshing to ensure our safety. We had our tricycles, toys, and a little table and chairs on the balcony, all of which were strategically placed around Mathew's carriage when he was with us, and from there we could almost touch the tree that was on our front lawn. It was our haven in the sky, as well as our window from our castle, which is what I imagined our house was. While we played there, we also talked to friends on the street and watched the activity across the road. There was an elementary school across the street, and we often heard the sound of children's voices as they played in the schoolyard.

The interior of our new house was also special. There were many rooms that branched out to the right and left of a sixty-foot-long hallway, and all the ceilings were about ten feet high. At the back end of the hallway, there was a large kitchen and at the other end, there was a den which led onto our balcony. All four of the bedrooms were on the left side of the hallway and on the right side was a living-room, which had a non-functional fireplace. There was also a dining-room, separated by French doors that miraculously slid into the walls; a breakfast nook, which was where we always ate, even though there were tables in both the dining-room and the kitchen; and a walk-in pantry just beside the kitchen. There were also two bathrooms in our house, one of these was a full bathroom, the other one just had a toilet. I loved this house because, despite its size, you could see most of the activity that was going on, as the house was all on one floor.

After we got settled into our new home, my mother had quite a job on her hands with three young children. However, she was still young, energetic, and somehow managed to have us all well-cared-for and occupied with interesting things to do. Although she hadn't planned to have another baby, when Mathew was only nine-months old, she became pregnant again. To her alarm, her doctor informed her at the beginning of her pregnancy that she had a large ovarian cyst and advised her to have an abortion. Nevertheless, despite her doctor's warnings, she decided to have her baby. Marc was born with no complications, even though he weighed nine pounds, and her cyst broke when he was delivered.

After Marc's birth, my mother decided to hire a live-in nurse to help her out for the first year, as she had previously done with me. The nurse took over many of the mundane and time consuming household chores, as well as helping to care for Marc, so that my mother could have more time to concentrate on her baby and still have some time left over to spend with the rest of us. I also helped my mother out by playing with Mathew and keeping him occupied during part of the day.

Because Marc had been born so soon after Mathew, I didn't respond to his arrival with the same interest as I had had towards Mathew's. I was so young myself – only four – and was still completely captivated by Mathew. Besides, by the time Marc became really receptive to others, at about nine months old, I had already found a real playmate in my brother Mathew.

Steven, on the other hand, was immediately taken with my brother Marc. It was as if this new baby had been brought to us especially for him, and Marc replaced me as the sibling Steven thought he had lost to Mathew. Although their age difference gave them very little in common, Marc was someone Steven could be affectionate with again, and right from the beginning, their relationship was special. They were similar in character, as were Mathew and I. Now my brothers and I appeared to be evenly paired off.

For four years, while Steven and I were in school, Mathew and Marc were at home together, and as a result they became very close, almost like twins in a way. Even though they did fight and had totally different characters, because they spent so much time together, Mathew and Marc became irreplaceable friends. Also, my mother had the time to help iron out their differences with them, as unfortunately she had never been able to do with my brothers and I when all of us were at home, which further strengthened their bond. The two boys shared the same room from the time that Marc was about one and a half years old.

Because the younger boys were always together, I became involved with both of them. I wanted to be with Mathew, but that meant Marc was usually around too--whether or not I wished him to be, and I found that very annoying. During this period, Steven was out of this group completely, as he was now so much older than us and busy with his own friends and activities. He and I were constantly bickering with each other anyway. From the time that I was as young as six years old, I can remember Steven teasing me and taunting me viciously, and, as the years passed, I understood his hostility even less. Perhaps it was because he resented my closeness to the two younger boys, and also his being left out of this threesome, but it never occurred to me at the time. I learned to dislike him, and was often afraid of him, but I never openly showed my fear for anger was acceptable in my family, whereas fear was ridiculed as a weakness or simply ignored. Because Steven continually tried to undermine my self-confidence, I tried to avoid him whenever I could.

During these early years, when we were small children, we spent a fair amount of time with our relatives. My mother's brother Siah had three sons, as did my father's brother Henry. The sisters-in-law were all good friends. Our family get-togethers were usually very gay, and I felt like we were a close-knit family, but, as we grew older, we saw one another less frequently. As children, my cousins and I were never encouraged to make plans to see one another on our own; it was only when our parents organized it that we saw each other. As a result, the boys' efforts at developing solid relationships with one another were stalemated. I used to wonder if the adults arranged these family meetings just for themselves, and that idea bothered me. I also disliked the way my parents compared all of us to one another after we arrived home.

Occasionally, we also went out as a family unit, to see a play or go to a movie, but, more often than not, to eat in restaurants. On these restaurant outings, Mom and Dad were especially proud of what an impressive group of kids we were. When we were quite young, we enjoyed going out to eat but, because my father was so impolite to the waitresses and to us, we became less and less fond of these outings as the years passed. Nevertheless, these family outings were our main source of recreation, because we never really relaxed together in the house. Our parents, especially our father, held the view that sitting around and doing nothing was the same as being useless. This was a concept that remained with us for life and it caused us a great deal of problems, as none of us ever learned to relax. We only participated in activities in smaller groups of two or three, never all six of us at once, except for the times when we went on family vacations. However, like our restaurant outings, because Dad didn't know how to enjoy himself around children, and was usually irritable, these trips became less successful with every passing year.

The only things we did do successfully as a group, and planned unselfishly for each individual family member, were birthday parties and other celebrations such as Mother's Day and Father's Day. On those special days, what we were habitually unable to express verbally on an affectionate level, we tried to make up for. We organized marvelous parties and made, or bought, beautiful cards and gifts. No one ever forgot anybody else, even when we were very young. Even though I thought these affectionate displays were often somewhat superficial, and unfortunately always too short-lived, nonetheless, our appreciation for one another as a family unit was reaffirmed on those days.

However, as far as our mother was concerned, there was no greater joy than being with her four children. She was our source of inspiration, encouragement, and guidance, and she devoted as much time as she could to ensure our development. For example, Mom always found the time to look at everything we created. She constantly praised us for all our individual talents and interests. I loved to draw – especially cartoons – I also wrote poetry and compositions, which were all considered quite exceptional skills for my age. Marc was an expert at figuring out how to take things apart and put them together again, everything from toys to small motors. Mathew demonstrated amazing athletic skills and was sports crazy. He was also extremely interested in world events and kept a scrapbook filled with newspaper clippings which he wrote commentaries about. We all thought that Mathew would end up being a professional athlete or a journalist. Steven was extremely interested in anything to do with the business world and had a remarkable aptitude for mathematics. All the boys collected stamps, baseball and hockey cards, and marbles; we were all interested in building things. Dad had given us a huge meccano set, with which we spent many enchanting hours creating fantasy lands.

Although our mother always encouraged us to develop these talents and interests, because she rarely spoke to us about emotions, she wasn't able to help us resolve our personal grievances – she was just incapable. Unfortunately, most of our childhood fights were left unresolved, and we often stopped only because we saw how much they upset her. However, my mother's failure to intervene often left us feeling confused and frustrated.

During these years, my father continued to work in his store six days a week, from nine in the morning until six at night. Thursday and Friday evenings, he worked until nine. Because work took up most of his time and energy, he began to resent our carefree existence and became progressively more agitated with my brothers and me.

He was managing his uncle's most important downtown store and had proved to be a brilliant salesman. His uncle kept a strong surveillance on everyone who worked for him, especially my father, and nothing my father ever did was good enough. He criticized my father's marketing plans, and told him that his displays were badly set up or that the cases weren't organized properly. He was never satisfied when my father produced amazing sales results that were based on Dad's ideas alone. He wouldn't give Dad any creative leverage, and although he had promised to help my father eventually acquire his own store, he sabotaged his nephew's every move towards autonomy. His uncle was a dreadful man, and from the time that Dad was fifteen years old, he had used my father as a scapegoat. Now that my father was married and had four small children, he knew that his nephew was truly dependent on him for employment. Because his uncle never followed up on his promise, my father's dreams of someday owning his own store were shattered. Although my mother encouraged him to leave his uncle's employ at any cost, that frightened him, and it was only when my father retired that he released himself from this horrendous man.

The frustrations of my father's daily plight and his subsequent rage over his Uncle's betrayal didn't show their full ugliness for some years to come – it was a gradual process. He spent the preliminary part of most evenings recounting to my mother how much he despised his uncle. Because he was stressed and short tempered due to the way he was being treated, he told fewer and fewer of his usual amusing stories. In addition, he was burdened by our presence, which, he made clear to my brothers and I, gave him a crowded feeling. He desperately needed my mother's emotional support to retain his sanity, but he couldn't get enough of her attention. She, on the other hand, desperately needed him to pay attention to us. Unlike my father, my mother seldom had the chance to air her own problems, such as the overwhelming job she had in caring for four small children, as there was no time for that. She was virtually raising us on her own, and I'm sure that sometimes she wasn't able to mask her frustration with my father for not severing his work ties. He, in turn, must have felt her disappointment in him, so it must have been a terrible predicament for both of them.

We learned everything about my father's work life and it's horrors by simply listening to his ranting, for my mother never explained to us the effects my uncle's behaviour had on him. This fit with her basic mode of silence, and it was also not usual for my parents' generation to communicate such things to their children. Therefore, being relatively ignorant of our father's plight, we showed little understanding of, or sympathy for, his hostilities towards us.

When we were very young, he had always been extremely playful and affectionate with us. Sometimes he'd have us laughing for what seemed like hours, embellishing his stories about customers into works of comedic art through his extraordinary sense of humour. Gradually, however, we saw his anger taking over. He played less frequently with us and would dismiss us as soon as we finished greeting him. His funny stories all but disappeared and were eventually replaced with angry recounts that we didn't understand.

My poor mother didn't really know what to do about all this. She made us go through the motions of greeting my father pleasantly when he arrived home, even though she knew that none of us were glad to see one another. Increasingly, he began to treat us like outsiders, with disdain and disrespect, as though our being there was more a necessary tolerance for him than a joy. His negative attitude towards us was beginning to damage our feelings of self-worth, and because he was critical and unpleasant and often picked fights with us from the moment he arrived home, we quickly learned to stay out of his way in order to avoid his verbal abuse.

Although Mom constantly tried to convince us that our father was interested in our accomplishments, we didn't believe her; he rarely asked to see anything we did and almost never gave praise, so we simply stayed out of his way. Eventually, I remember watching the clock with dread as the hour approached for his arrival. I knew that the moment he would walk through the door, the atmosphere of harmony in our home would end. I often thought that he didn't want us, and was convinced that he didn't like us. Yes, he loved us, but he only showed it occasionally and it was seldom unconditional. Although he sometimes supported us, it always included some criticism. My father expected excellence from all of us, but invested very little time in advising us how to achieve this goal, and when we did excel, he never showed any appreciation for our fine work. Even though my mother listened to him and supported him through his endless problems at work, she fought with my father for years over his unjust transferal of anger on to his innocent children. He had no idea of the potentially irreversible damage he was inflicting on us all. She tried to have us do things to please him, but our hearts weren't in it and none of them worked. Nothing we did was ever good enough for him, and, although he didn't realize it, he was doing to us exactly what his uncle had done, and was continuing to do, to him.

Despite the fact that my father spent so little time at home, his influence on the formation of our characters was astounding. The effects were far worse on the boys, particularly for Steven because he fought back. However, Dad wasn't nearly as abusive towards me as he was towards my brothers. Although he often made inane remarks in reference to the fact that I was a girl, which was inexcusable to me, we still had occasional affectionate moments with each other. The way that he treated the boys, especially when he would turn on Mathew, really upset me, and, as a result of this, my father and I became estranged as well.

Marc despised Dad in his own quiet way by casting hateful glances at him. Mathew was both afraid of Dad and hurt by his abuse, and although he was confused by Dad's behaviour, rather than hating him for it, he forgave him. I was both afraid and angry at the same time, but I somehow found a little compassion for what I perceived to be a tortured man, whom we all once openly loved and whom my mother loved still.

However, despite my father's erratic behaviour, he did give us a certain sense of security. He always came home at night, never had a drinking problem, and never demonstrated an interest in other women. He had a strong moral character and took his responsibilities seriously, and for this we had a great respect for him. However, it was mainly because our parents' marriage was visibly solid that we survived Dad's mood swings.

He and Mom were quite romantic at times. As he had done before they were married, he continued to bring her lovely gifts even when there was no special occasion. He teased her affectionately and flirted with her openly, and I especially enjoyed the way he looked at her, and still does look at her, in that loving and passionate way that usually wears off after the first few years of marriage. He would often remark about how beautiful and intelligent he thought she was, but what I enjoyed best of all was the way he could still make her laugh.

Nevertheless, the relationships between my brothers and I became more and more affected by the tumultuous existence we were experiencing by living with my father. We had fallen into negative patterns of behaviour towards one another which should have been changed, but our parents didn't have the time or the energy to redirect us. Steven and Marc developed both hot and cold personalities; they were either very funny and very charming, or very serious and very unpleasant. They were also often quiet and sullen, especially Marc, as they both inherited my mother's silent manner. On the other hand, Mathew and I had more positive personalities, as neither of us became angry, cold, or temperamental over the years. We were both a bit loud and aggressive at times, but we were never intentionally unkind.

Steven related well to both the boys, but, although he found Mathew to be happy-go-lucky and talented, he obviously preferred Marc. However, my relationship with Steven grew progressively worse as the years passed. Because I never realized that he despised me for not being victimized by Dad as much as he was, I felt that his hostility was completely undeserved. He learned from my father's example to treat me in exactly the same way that Dad treated him. Steven's animosity towards me left me feeling confused and overly sensitive whenever he was around, and because my mother wasn't trying to change or correct his behaviour towards me, I began to resent her for it. Perhaps she felt this would only compound the problem, for apparently Steven perceived my relationship with Mom as something special and enviable. It never occurred to Steven that, as the only girl in the house, I often felt lonely and that, in actuality, I was not receiving the proper consideration, not even from Mom.

Even though Steven often rejected me, Mathew and Marc appreciated my presence. Because Mathew was a much warmer person, I wanted to be with him more than I wanted to be with Marc. Although it was apparent to Marc that I preferred Mathew to him, Marc still wanted to be with me, and, therefore, he seemed to accept my insensitivity towards him. I felt guilty about how I treated him, but I wasn't able to change this situation. Despite my preference, and because Mathew always encouraged me to include Marc in our activities together, Marc didn't resent Mathew for this favoured position with me. However, Marc resented me for it, and unbeknown to me, that resentment was growing and festering in him. Furthermore, I deluded myself into believing that Steven's special affection for Marc somehow compensated for this, but I was wrong.

Mathew was the only brother who appreciated the fact that I was a girl. When I was dressed up, he always noticed and told me how pretty I looked. He used to tease me that even though I wasn't endowed with his beautiful skin, he considered mine to be quite lovely too. I remember watching the Miss Canada Pageant one evening with my whole family. The next day, Mathew mentioned to me that he considered me to be as attractive and as talented as any of the contestants, and it was comments like this that endeared him to me. He loved the idea of having a sister, or at least he made me feel that way. He loved me just because I was there, and I wasn't required to prove anything in order to receive his love. No one else in the house made me feel accepted or special the way Mathew did, not even my parents.

Mathew had an innocent and cheerful comportment. Besides being a warm and receptive person, he was the only one among us that related well to everyone. Steven liked and admired him, Marc loved him, and I simply adored him. My often barely tolerable relationship with Steven, my lukewarm relationship with Marc, my lack of a close connection with Mom, and Dad's inconsistent behaviour were all quite bearable because of my feelings for Mathew. As he was the only person in the house that I was in complete harmony with, he gave me just about everything I needed emotionally. It didn't even matter to me that I was not as important to him as he was to me. He was there for me, and as long as he was, I never felt alone.

When Steven was fourteen, I was ten, Mathew was eight, and Marc was six years old, my parents announced to us that we were all moving to the north end of the city and into a beautiful new house of our own. The money required for the down payment for this new home came from the funds my mother had set aside when she sold her share of the slipper business to her brother Sam, as along with all the money my parents had managed to save over the years. Even though this meant that my parents would have nothing left to fall back on, my mother insisted on the move.

However, my brothers and I hardly shared our parent's enthusiasm, for we found the new neighbourhood strange and ugly. Instead of our beautiful maples, all the lawns had newly planted trees, which looked like twigs, on them, and there was no school across the street, only a field. There were no stores anywhere in sight. In our new house, there were three bedrooms upstairs. My parents slept in one, Mathew and Marc shared another, and I was in the third. Steven was separated from us, two floors down in his own room. Although I wondered whether he liked this arrangement or whether he felt left out, because we fought so much, I was glad not to have him close by.

I didn't feel attached to this new house the way I did to the one in Outremont, but because I thought they would think I was selfish and unappreciative, I didn't express my feelings to either my parents or my brothers. For the first time in my life, I was unhappy about where I lived.

Within one year of this move, my mother decided to return to work. She was forty years old and for the first time she had to look for work outside of her family's business, but, because she was a fully qualified bookkeeper, she found a job easily. Although my father wholly objected to the idea of my mother working, she knew that relieving my father of some of the financial burden would make everyone's lives easier.

While our mother worked, my brothers and I continued to pursue all our special interests and to indulge in our usual antics together. Mathew and Marc both had paper routes, Marc's was before school and Mathew's was after school. The two of them played table-top hockey, and we all played ping-pong together downstairs in the basement. Mathew and Marc made model airplanes and cars, Mathew and I did number paintings, and we all played games like Monopoly, Scrabble, and cards. Occasionally, we would make cookie batter before Mom got home, then eat most of it before it got baked. In winter we skated on the rink across the street, and in summer we rode our bikes around the block, seeing who could ride the longest without touching the handle bars. Our playtime antics also included wrestling on our beds or on the floor, and games such as "airplane." In the latter, I'd lie flat on my back, then hold their hands and push my brothers up in the air by placing my feet on their thighs.

Mom never complained about how difficult the transition from home to office must have been for her. We all did our best to help her out, especially Steven, who, as always, felt responsible for us children and for Mom. My brothers and I showed our appreciation for her efforts by doing chores without being asked and always greeting her lovingly when she arrived home. However, despite all our good intentions, we would still ask if our supper was ready within five minutes of her arrival home.

Just before we moved from Outremont, we celebrated Steven's Bar Mitzvah which was the most special occasion we ever had in our first home. I was only nine years old at the time, Mathew was seven, and Marc was four. I remember preparing sumptuous food displays with Mom and the caterers and how beautiful all the decorations and flower arrangements looked. I also remember how I loved the new, powder-blue, chiffon dress that Mom bought me for the occasion. Although, I can recall no special feelings about the day itself other than being proud of Steven, nor can I remember anything about the ceremony at the synagogue.

The first really big celebration to be held in our new home was Mathew's Bar Mitzvah. It was held in January of 1963, a few weeks after his thirteenth birthday. Perhaps it is because either I was older, or so much fonder of Mathew than I was of Steven, but I remember every moment and detail of this event. Mathew, like all other boys who are to be Bar Mitzvahed, had to learn a portion from the Scriptures, which he would then have to chant during the Saturday Sabbath services in front of the entire congregation in the synagogue. In order to learn how to chant the scripture properly, he took lessons from a Cantor for a few months. According to his teacher, Mathew thoroughly enjoyed this exercise and was a joy to tutor.

I can still see Mathew standing there at the podium. The sun was shining through the windows on to the Ark where he stood, and the way the sunlight fell around him, illuminating his blonde hair and white silk Tallis, it made him look like an angel. Without a flaw, he chanted calmly and proudly. The Cantor came over to my parents after the service and told them that he had been in awe of Mathew during the ceremony, and many other people echoed this sentiment in their congratulatory remarks. Mathew accepted their congratulations without any childish vanity, and our family was astonished with the way he conducted himself that day.

A few months later, there was another celebration that made a lasting impression on me. Mathew had talked Steven into driving him and Mom to the Stagecoach Inn Restaurant. It was Mother's Day and Mathew had been saving his allowance and earnings from his paper route just for this occasion. He asked the rest of the family if we wouldn't mind his taking Mom out alone after we had all given her our gifts, which we all thought was a charming idea, and subsequently made the restaurant reservations himself.

When they arrived home, my mother told us how Mathew had acted like a perfect gentleman during the luncheon. He had pulled out her chair for her, ordered the food, and paid for the bill just like an adult would have, and the restaurant staff told my mother how impressed they had been with him as well. It was amazing how refined at times this rough and tumble boy could be. My mother said that it was one of the happiest and most memorable occasions of her life. Unknown to her, however, it was to be her last with my brother Mathew.

4

THE DEATH

It was the afternoon of May 21, 1963, only ten days after Mother's Day. Marc was busy doing homework in his room, and Steven was downstairs reading a book. My father wasn't home from work yet, and my mother was preparing supper in the kitchen. Mathew wanted to play baseball out in front of the house, but none of us felt like playing, so he asked my mother if he could go to the park to watch a baseball game. She said it would be alright as long as he was back by eight or so. It was six o'clock when Mathew left on his bike.

My father arrived home at about six-thirty and ate supper alone with my mother, as my brothers and I had already eaten. At around eight-fifteen, my parents started to get agitated because Mathew wasn't home yet. He was habitually punctual and, unlike most other children, never stayed out longer than he was supposed to. By eight-forty-five he still wasn't home, and we were all becoming frantic. My father and Steven went out in the car to look for Mathew, but they returned about a half an hour later without him. By this time, my mother was becoming hysterical. As we all tried to calm her, my father called the police to report Mathew as missing.

While we waited for the police to arrive at our house, I remember that a feeling of doom came over me. As non-religious as I was, I knelt in front of a living-room chair, praying for the life of my brother. The doorbell rang and my father answered it. There were two policemen standing there, and they asked if my father was Mr. Roth. He hesitated and then added in a most sympathetic tone, "Mr. Roth, I deeply regret to have to inform you that your son has been involved in a fatal accident."

My father staggered backwards into the foyer, crying out, "No! No! No!" The policeman's words were like a knife that stabbed him, for I had never seen such an expression of pain on his face before. Although he was only forty-five years old and in prime health, at that moment he looked small, frail, and beaten. My mother started shrieking that it had to be a mistake, that the child they were speaking of couldn't be her Mathew.

The policemen produced a large brown envelope and emptied the contents on to the dining-room table. The envelope contained everything that Mathew had with him when he left the house that afternoon including his glasses, his keys, some change, his wallet, and a few other treasured little things that all children carry around with them. There before our eyes was the truth, but even though I saw Mathew's belongings, I told myself it wasn't true.

I started screaming – it felt like my head would explode. I saw myself running wildly, trying to get away from my house. Then there seemed to be no walls or earth or sky, and I was falling through a whirling void. I blacked out momentarily, but, to my horror, when I came to I was still there. The pain was so intense that I wanted to die. I couldn't live without Mathew. What was I going to do? I was bonded to him in a way that no one understood and I couldn't imagine life without him – I didn't want life without him.

One of the policemen came and shook me out of my hysteria so that I could try and help my parents. My father sat on a chair, limp and weeping; my mother sat on the red couch in the living room, sobbing uncontrollably. I sat on the stairs and faced her from across the foyer, witnessing the physical and spiritual metamorphosis that such news could cause. The glitter, the beauty, and the happiness of my mother's youth dissolved before my eyes, and to this day they have never returned. I remember her looking up and there was something terrible in her eyes. It was an expression beyond grief, a hateful, be-trayed-by-life look. It really frightened me because I felt like we had lost her as well.

The police stayed at our house for a long time, until, finally, my father and Steven went with them to identify Mathew's body at the morgue in case it was some terrible error. In case, God willing, he had been abducted, or critically injured, or anything but dead. However, they returned home with the dreaded confirmation. It had been a freak accident. Although the car had been going very slowly, neither the driver nor Mathew saw one another until the moment that Mathew had been lightly struck down. He fell from his bicycle on to the sidewalk and was killed instantly. He had suffered a fatal blow to his temple, but the peculiar thing about it was that he didn't have a scratch on his body – there wasn't even a bruise from the fall! The rest of that fateful evening is still a blur to me, although I do recall that no one in the family slept. We all seemed to be walking around with blank expressions on our faces, especially Marc, who had the same large, vacant eyes as my mother's.

Steven stayed with my parents to discuss the funeral arrange-ments. They had to be made quickly, for it is customary in the Jewish tradition to bury the dead within two days. Steven contacted my Uncle Henry, who arrived early the next morning. Henry, my aunt Rhoda, and Steven helped organize everything with my parents because my mother and father were almost completely helpless.

It was early the following morning when our family left for the funeral home to see Mathew for the last time. As we approached the viewing chamber, I felt as if I couldn't breathe. In my mind, I imag-ined myself trying to escape. I saw the viewing chamber retreating further and further away from me, so that I would never be able to reach it and therefore not have to go through with this. The door of the room opened and everything I was imagining stopped.

All I could see was my family members hunched over, sobbing bit-terly; it was then that I experienced agony for the first time in my life. As we took our last look at our beloved Mathew, I couldn't believe the striking contrast between the tortured, exhausted faces of all of us, and the peaceful, rested face of our Mathew. Even in death, he had that ever-present hint of a smile on his lips.

For a moment I thought of the mortician who had prepared his body and I shuddered. I etched the sight of Mathew's glistening blonde hair, his velvet skin, and his well-formed hands into my memory. I almost went over and embraced him, for I couldn't believe that anyone who looked so vibrant could possibly be dead. As I backed away from this physical part of him, I could see a radiance around his coffin that I somehow knew was his spirit, and that meant he was still with us.

After taking one last look, we had to support one another physically as we left the viewing chamber. We walked downstairs to the main salon where the eulogy was to take place. The rabbi from our synagogue spoke briefly and with great compassion about Mathew. While he spoke, I looked up for a moment and saw that the hall was packed with people, many of whom I didn't recognize. I remember wishing all through the eulogy that it had been me who died instead of Mathew, but I was alive and therefore my torment continued. I thought for a moment about the freak car accident that had killed him, and vowed to myself that I would kill the driver of that car if I could ever regain my senses enough to plan it. I denounced God for taking Mathew away from us and for subjecting my family to such anguish. I remember feeling that nothing would ever be the same between any of us again, for I could already feel the change that was taking place. Rather than uniting us, this tragedy was separating us. I knew this situation would never be corrected, and all during the service my grief was compounded immeasurably by this knowledge.

After Mathew was put into the hearse, the family and everyone else who had attended the funeral got into their respective automobiles and drove to the cemetery. We all arrived there within half an hour and walked slowly to the plot. The rabbi, who conducted the burial service, spoke lovingly of Mathew. He had known my brother personally because he had been the presiding rabbi at Mathew's recent Bar Mitzvah. My parents, my brothers, and I opened our prayer books and read from the traditional last rites. First my parents spoke:

Sweetly slumber, the darling of my heart rests here –

my dear, early departed child, peace onto this soul –

God of grace and mercy, forgive the depressed heart

of a parent trembling in unutterable woe ... for I had

hoped that his hand would close my eyes...

I was filled with loathing for these words because I felt they were such cruel words, asking my parents to be forgiven for their grief and encouraging them into a state of silence.

My brothers and I began to recite our passages, but, after the first few words, we were unable to go on; so the rabbi had to read them aloud for us:

May peace be thine, dear friend of my youth.

What gentle memories and bitter regret

cluster around this tomb. Alas! death

claimed thee too soon and removed thee too

early from those who loved thee. What

grief! to think that we, whom one roof

sheltered, one mother nourished, the same

hearts cherished and the same hands blessed,

are forever separated.

We were so happy together; thy friendship

was so sweet a support. Alas! thy departure

has turned our joy into mourning.

Nothing on earth is lasting...

I held no malice for these words. I felt they accurately represented Mathew and our feelings about him, and it was as if they had been extracted from our very thoughts.

Then we buried him. As they lowered Mathew's coffin into the earth, I felt that any hope for our family's happiness was being buried with him, and I doubted if that hope could ever be retrieved. Overwhelmed by grief at having had to witness the burial of a child, everybody left the cemetery in silence.

According to the Gideon's Bible, verses twenty-one and twenty-two in the Book of Revelations are Glimpses of Heaven and the Glory of God. Two years ago for no apparent reason, my mother gave me Mathew's diary from school, and I discovered that on the day before Mathew's death, he had to study the Book of Revelations as part of his homework, chapter twenty-one, verses one through four and verse twenty-two. Verse one comes just before the Apocalypse and begins with the following, "And I saw a new heaven and a new earth, for the first heaven and the first earth passed away and there is no longer any sea." The fourth verse reads, "He shall wipe away every tear from their eyes: and there shall no longer be any death; there shall no longer be any mourning, or crying, or pain; the first things have passed away."

The words in these verses are in reference to God's existence, His power, and to the assurance of the next life. What is strange is that, despite my hard and fast denouncement of God for so many years, they gave me comfort in some way. What's also odd is that Mathew read these words just before his death; and it's ironic that, although verse four of The Revelations marked the end of sorrow for Mathew, it marked the beginning of sorrow for the rest of our family.

After a death in the family, it is a tradition of our faith to have what is called a Shiva, or a period of mourning, which lasts for about a week. All the mirrors are covered in the house, the men don't shave, and the bereaved family doesn't cook meals or leave their home. The purpose of the Shiva is to give spiritual support. The rabbi spends several hours a day praying with the immediate family, close relatives, and friends. Also, relatives and friends bring food and try their best to console the parents and children of the family involved.

During the week of Mathew's Shiva, Steven's girlfriend came to the house almost every day, which provided him emotional support. However, neither Marc's nor my friends came to see us, as Marc's friends were too young and my friends didn't know how to approach me. My younger brother and I desperately needed our parents to comfort us, but they were oblivious to our pain. They were lost in their own anguish, especially my mother, who had retreated so far into herself that no one could reach her, not even my father. She cried all the time, and Steven, Marc, and I didn't have any idea of how to try and help her. We wanted to alleviate her torment, but her eyes gave off the impression that she didn't want to be touched or talked to.

For the first few days of the Shiva, I spent most of my time alone in my room because I couldn't bear watching my parents and my relatives praying and weeping in the living-room. On the afternoon of the third day, I decided to go downstairs to the den, where I found Steven and his girlfriend alone, embracing in silence. I became outraged and told them it was not the occasion to be in each other's arms, and then ran upstairs to my room. My brother followed after me, outraged by my reaction. He slapped me and then left in tears.

It was the first instance since Mathew's funeral in which I saw Steven lose control and allow himself to express his pain.

Due to the shock of this experience, I ran out of the house and on to the front lawn. It was the first time in three days that I went outside. I leaned on our linden tree and caught sight of a neighbour who was one of my school friends, watching me from across the street. We both stood frozen, staring at each other. After what seemed to be an eternity, she took one furtive step forward, when I started screaming, then collapsed. My friend instantly ran away. Steven must have been watching me because he immediately rushed out, picked me up, carried me into the house, and brought me back to my room.

Marc also stayed in his room during the Shiva, except for the times when he was called downstairs to eat. He didn't want to see or speak to anyone, for, like my mother, he was in a total state of shock and completely unresponsive.

I withdrew into myself, having decided that my loss was greater than anyone else's in the family. How could anyone understand what Mathew had meant to me? Perhaps my mother could have, but I made up my mind that my brothers definitely could not; however, I kept all these feelings to myself. How grateful I am now that I had the ignorance of my youth to blame for these distorted sentiments. However, my withdrawal from my brothers did not go unpaid for, as they somehow knew how I felt and never really forgave me.

After all our relatives and visitors had left, the evenings of the Shiva were intolerably quiet. My mother had trouble sleeping and my father would be woken up every night because of her nightmares. In her sleep, Mom rambled on about wanting to die and about wanting to be buried next to Mathew. Dad tried to calm her down, but she didn't respond.

I couldn't sleep either and would go downstairs to the kitchen, where I would sit alone in the dark. On a couple of these nights, my father also came down to the kitchen and found me there. He would tell me about how helpless he felt about being unable to comfort my mother. I wanted so much to ease his pain, but I also hated him for every unkind word he had ever uttered to Mathew unjustly. Nevertheless, my feelings of compassion were stronger. I listened to him and kept my resentful thoughts buried inside myself, for these were the only incidents of any real communication about Mathew's death that I ever had with anyone in my family during this week of mourning.

On one of these nights with my father, he said something deeply profound to me. He said, "Laura, I have found out that just to live, with most everything going right – with good health, work going well, and my wife and children taken care of – it is still not easy. When something like this happens, you want to give up living because it makes life almost impossible to bear." Now that I am close to the age that he was when he spoke these words, I realize how right he was. It is hard sometimes just to go on living with ourselves.

After that evening, with the exception of my father who constantly tried to share his grief with my mother, no one else talked to one another about Mathew, or held one another, or cried together. It was as if we were strangers, and the only thing common to us all was our loss, our torment, and our guilt.

Although we felt it was the most agonizing week of our lives, the real torment lay ahead of us. After the Shiva was over, we were all by ourselves, the calls tapered off and everyone thought that if they left us alone long enough, things would return to normal. However, they never did.

5

THE AFTERMATH-LIFE WITHOUT MATHEW

As I lay in my dark room at night, all I could think about was Mathew in that coffin – Matthew in an unfamiliar place, surrounded by those unfamiliar bodies. In my mind I had not really accepted the fact that Mathew was dead, or the concept of his spirit having been released from his body. I thought of him deteriorating in that coffin, and that thought was unbearable. I wanted to go and dig the coffin up to see if he still looked like my Mathew, to see if he still looked peaceful and had that same glow that surrounded him when I last saw him. This kind of thinking really distressed me and deepened my growing fears. I was suddenly afraid of everything – the present, the future. I never had so many pronounced fears before we lost Mathew, or else they hadn't showed themselves before this. Even worse, I hid all these fears, as my family never supported any debility in anyone, especially their children. If demonstrated, these fears would be disregarded, or set aside as weakness, and weakness was completely unacceptable to them. This reaction was the basis of my anger towards my family, because I never felt that they took me seriously.

I also couldn't bear the front I had to put up due to their total lack of sympathy, or their inability to recognize my state of terror. And, because they didn't accept my fears, I found them exceedingly difficult to accept in myself. It was no wonder I always felt trapped and confused and that I decided the only way out was to die. Although I considered that option for a few years, I was afraid to kill myself because I thought of the grief it would cause my parents. Even in my thoughts of suicide, my parents were interfering. It was always them, never me. I felt no comfort at all in their pseudo concern, and because their neglect and denial was ruining my life, I decided that as soon as I had an opportunity to do so, I would get away from them.

Soon after Mathew's death, my mother busied herself with gathering all of Mathew's things together – his clothes, his books, his photos, his personal belongings – everything. Although I never knew what she did with his belongings, the pictures of him were put away somewhere in her room, along with a few other cherished items.

I don't recall exactly when they removed Mathew's bed and furniture from his and Marc's room, but they did. This was done in order to make it possible for Marc to bear staying in that room alone. However, this didn't work out, as he found it too depressing to stay there, and subsequently had to be moved. My parents asked me if I would do Marc the favour of switching rooms with him. I was delighted with the idea, because I felt it was a privilege to be in the room where Mathew had spent so much of his time. Marc agreed to take my room, even though it was much smaller than his, for it looked out on to the front yard of the house. Once it was repainted in the colour of his choice, he moved into it and felt much better. And, once it was ready for me, I gladly settled into my new room because it was filled with memories of Mathew. I would envision his beautiful, smiling face in front of me as I lay on my bed. This vision preoccupied my sleepless nights for months, until I would finally drift off from exhaustion.

I was the one elected to go to Mathew's school to collect his possessions. Although I was reluctant, my parents and Steven were incapable of going, and, of course, Marc was too young. From the moment I walked into the school, I remember how awkward everyone acted towards me. Everywhere I could hear children whispering, "That's Mathew's sister. The principal told me to wait for her in the gym while she gathered everything together. She brought Mathew's things to me without saying a word, and after she left I stayed in the gym, sitting on a small bench.

While I sat there, I suddenly noticed there was a rehearsal for a play going on featuring the kindergarten and grade-one children. Mathew and Marc had performed in similar productions. At that moment, there was a six-year-old boy on the stage who was blonde, round-faced, and confident. I became overwhelmed with the memory of Mathew, and I broke down and started sobbing. As several teachers advanced toward me, I got up, ran out of the school, and down the street - blind with tears – clutching my parcel until I reached home.

I composed myself as best as I could before I went in, gave the parcel to my mother, and disappeared upstairs into my room. I could not bear to see her anguished face, nor for her to be further burdened by my tears. Although I felt she should have, she never asked me about this traumatic incident. It was over with, but I never forgave her for having sent me to do this task.

It had been since a month before Mathew's death that I'd gone out with my boyfriend Ronnie. Even though I had no desire for his or anyone else's company, one night I finally agreed to go to a movie with him. We decided to see Tammy Tell Me True starring Sandra Dee. However, it turned out to be an immature, overdramatized children's story, and there was one scene in it that was upsetting enough to ruin the whole evening for me. In the scene, Sandra Dee was on the beach imploring God to save her grandmother's life. I was appalled and unable to feel even a bit of sympathy. I ran out of the theatre and on to the street. Ronnie came running after me, wanting to know what was wrong, but I couldn't explain and just asked him to take me home. We didn't say a word to one another all the way there.

When we arrived, I told him I was sorry, and excused myself quickly. I ran up the front stairs and into the house. My parents were still up when I got home. I made up some excuse for arriving so early, and then calmly and quietly made my way to my room. Once there, I let myself go, muffling my sobs in my pillow so that no one would hear me, a reaction that I was unfortunately becoming accustomed to. It was then that I realized something terrible was happening to me, which I had not been fully aware of until now. Ever since Mathew's death, I had a complete absence of sympathy or compassion for anyone else's pain. I had become indifferent because I felt that no one else's misery could possibly compare with mine. It never occurred to me that other people suffered a similar misfortune. Furthermore, I realized that I had been lost in my own anger and had expressed this anger through a silent smugness, which included a denouncing of God and a masked coldness for other people's misfortunes.

Going back to school was the hardest thing I had to do since going to Mathew's funeral. I already felt isolated because Josie, who had been my closest bosom buddy and constant companion for over four years, had moved to Toronto the year before, so I was very alone to begin with. After Josie moved away, I was friendly with my peers, but since the time of Mathew's death I hadn't been particularly friendly with anyone.

Everyone in school avoided me. Teenagers are ill-equipped to deal with emotional stress, let alone the trauma of dealing with a friend who has just lost a brother. Every day I had to deal with my classmates' sad gazes and awkward conversations. Neither they nor my teachers could speak to me comfortably. To escape everyone's doleful looks, I would often wander around the school hallways during classes. My teachers tolerated this behaviour patiently, as did Mr. Thomas, the principal. Occasionally, Mr. Thomas accompanied me in silence, which was his way of telling me that he sympathized with my situation.

It was the beginning of June and final exams were imminent, but I couldn't concentrate at all on my schoolwork. It was only because of my previous scholastic record that my teachers passed me that year. I remember one very disturbing incident from that last month in school. I left the building during lunch hour and walked over to the synagogue our family frequented, which was only a few blocks away. It was the same synagogue that Mathew had been Bar Mitzvahed in. I entered the empty chapel and sat staring at the eternal light set above the Ark, which contained the Torahs. I became overwhelmed with a hatred for God, and started screaming at Him and cursing Him for taking Mathew from me. The janitor came in and helped me out of the chapel, and although he said nothing he, stayed with me until I calmed down. I don't recall returning to school that day, but my parents never found out about the incident, nor did anyone else for that matter, because I told nobody until many years after. I was starting to believe that no one would ever be able to help me and therefore I didn't let myself express my pain again for a very long time.

When the school year ended, a month had passed since Mathew had been killed. During the entire summer that followed, our family pretended everything was reasonably normal. My father worked as usual and my mother tried to recuperate. Steven had just completed his second year at university and found himself a summer job, and Marc spent most of his time with his friends. I retreated alone to the back yard to think about Mathew and to wonder how I was going to survive what I foresaw as a bleak future in front of me.

I had not been prepared for the absolute loneliness and sense of abandonment I was feeling since we lost Mathew. My relationships with my brothers were strained and my parents were in the depths of despair, and because of this I felt like I had lost everyone. None of us ever spoke about Mathew, even though the gloom created by his absence hung heavy on us.

During the summer months, we were especially considerate of my mother. Mom, the once energetic pillar of strength upon whom we had always depended on, was now weak and fragile, so my brothers and I took it upon ourselves to become the custodians of my mother's broken heart. Just as comparing other people's misfortunes to your own does not provide any lasting comfort, trying to help our mother overcome her grief, with no one helping us in return, left us even further from overcoming ours. She never effectively even started to recover, as she wouldn't let herself be helped. I felt no relief whether she improved or not, and I felt no less distraught because her loss was considered worse than ours, even though it was. She just wasn't there for us anymore. It was so unfair. We children were entitled to express our own pain, for our own sake without having to compare it to our parents'. Although my brothers and I were learning how to live with our parents' silence, it was working itself into my anger, resentment, and guilt, in the deepest sense. I was angry at my mother, but at the same time I felt guilty over that anger. I was also angry at my father for every moment of healing time that I imagined he stole from me by taking up my mother's every spare minute for himself when he was home.

Once he had gained enough strength back to function at work, my father's manner towards my brothers and I returned to the way it had always been. For a long time, he no longer had my mother to listen to him talk about his problems. His life situation was still as frustrating as it had been prior to Mathew's death. Now, because my mother was in such a weak emotional condition, this only added to his difficulties. In addition, he had to deal with the guilt he must have felt for all the abuse he had ever given Mathew, as well as the knowledge that he would never have the chance to say he was sorry.

All of us tried to a pay some extra attention to Marc because he was the youngest child, and also because Mathew's absence affected him more directly than any of us, as he and Mathew had been roommates. When my father occasionally bothered Marc, my mother always came to Marc's defence, but despite this, even at the age of twelve, I often heard Marc vow that as soon as he could, he would leave home. This amazed me as I always felt apprehensive about being on my own, even though living at home now made me feel helpless and trapped. I was afraid to go anywhere else and I always envied the early confidence Marc displayed about leaving.

Steven dove into his summer job with a great passion and occupied his leisure time reading business magazines and stock-market reviews. He bought an expensive car that he couldn't afford and went out at night far too often. In other words, he kept himself so busy that he had no time to think. He spent some time with Marc whenever he could fit it in to his hectic schedule. However, Steven and I continued to argue over everything, and my father and he grew progressively more vicious towards one another. I believe that the only reason Steven didn't move out of the house at this time was because he was so worried about my mother. I was anxious to get back to school after the summer of relative solitude for I had spent far too much time thinking about Mathew. I wanted to call or write Josie in Toronto, to tell her about Mathew's accident, but I couldn't muster up the courage.

The nights continued to be the worst times for me. I stopped seeing my boyfriend Ronnie and I had no desire to go out with anyone else, so I read a great deal and brooded alone in my room. I would cry myself to sleep every night, or else I would torment myself for hours, lying awake and wondering what everyone else in the family was feeling about our situation. I would think about Marc and how I would watch him, without him knowing, as he went about his business in the house. I noticed how he withdrew into himself in a way that a stranger might perceive was an independent nature. I knew he was in pain. I knew he was screaming inside like I was, but, because I never had the same affection for him as I had for Mathew, I didn't know how to approach him.

I missed that union with Mathew – that daily, ever-present union. I tried to imagine developing it with Marc, but in my own tortured mind I looked at him with both love and hate. I loved him just for being alive and for being my brother, and, therefore, understanding my pain as I understood his. However, I also hated him for being alive, when Mathew was —not – then I hated myself for having such thoughts. How lost he must have been without his other-half. They had been so meshed together, and as different as they were, being without Mathew must have been like walking without a leg for Marc. Although I felt guilty about not telling him how I sympathized with his loss, because I was so emotionally debilitated myself, I couldn't. I'm sure that he took my silence as a rejection never faulted through my telling him that it wasn't so. The odd time I caught sight of his frozen, furtive glance, I was terrified to talk to him about any of this, so I let these opportunities pass and never said anything.

Then there were my thoughts about Steven. I tried to block the recurring image of what it must have been like to be only twenty years old and have to identify the dead body of his younger brother. I also wondered what it must have been like to have to pretend to be strong at that moment for our parents' sake, when his own strength had been knocked right out of him. Worst of all, I wondered if Steven had helped pick out the clothes that Mathew wore in his coffin. God! How did he ever survive that? He was still only a boy himself, and I wondered how the trauma of this experience would affect him. I never told Marc or Steven about those sleepless nights, when I lay awake thinking about them, because I was afraid to ask them how they felt about Mathew's death, and they never once offered to tell me anything, either.

Steven and I had not been close for years, and because we avoided each other during these summer months, we drifted even further apart. He was concerned about Marc, as were my parents, but Steven and I were no one's concern. Perhaps my aloofness made him feel that I didn't care about him. His demeanour of self-control really irritated me. I despised him for it, not realizing at the time that it was a cover-up. He never knew how I grieved over his hidden tears, or how I needed to hold him, weep with him, and talk to him about my anguish. Only Steven and Marc knew how I felt, no one else could. However, my brothers and I never reached out to one another. We pretended to ourselves that we were healing but in reality we were getting worse because we held everything inside.

I'm sure that it never occurred to my parents how their silence was affecting us. I sometimes had the dreadful thought that perhaps they wished it had been one of us instead of Mathew, and I believe that Steven and Marc must have felt that way, as well. I'm convinced my parents didn't have any idea that we ever entertained such thoughts.

6

SPLITTING APART

After the summer that I passed in relative solitude, I was anxious to get back to school, for I spent far too much time thinking about Mathew. A few weeks after I started grade eleven, I managed to secure a friend whom I could finally bear to be with. Heidi was new in school, having just moved to Montreal a few months before, and didn't know anything about our tragedy. Although I did eventually tell her about Mathew, she had recently lost her father and didn't want to be constantly reminded of her own loss, either. Because we understood each other's need for anonymity, we became each other's companions for that year; and if it hadn't been for Heidi, I don't know how I would have made it through my last year in high school.

While I was in grade eleven, I managed to do something else which I felt was a step in the right direction. In April, I went to Toronto for a couple of days to visit my friend Josie, whereby I rid myself of some of the heavy burden that I had been carrying inside of me for so long. During the summer months, I wanted to call or write Josie to tell her about Mathew's accident, but I couldn't muster up the courage. In Toronto, however, I opened up to her and because she had also known and loved Mathew, it was a great release.

Unfortunately, this release was brief. Shortly after my trip to Toronto, the month of May arrived, and with it an event that I had long been dreading. My family and I were all required to go to the cemetery to unveil Mathew's tombstone, another tradition in our faith. At the unveiling, all the horror of his death was relived in our minds. We left the graveyard in a shocked and anguished state, without a —word – as if we were strangers.

During the month of June, my family deliberated on whether or not Marc should go to a sleeping-camp or whether or not we thought he would be too lonely if he did go. Finally, Marc insisted on going and he spent part of the summer in a camp up north. While Marc was at camp, my parents went to Florida for a few weeks and left Steven and I in charge of the house.

The summer passed quickly for my brothers and me. Steven was overloaded with work and I went to a day-camp for several weeks. Before we knew it, by the time Marc had returned home at the end of August, it was September again and the beginning of another school year.

When I started university I had a more staggered schedule than I had had in high school, which I appreciated. I was also grateful for the anonymity of I gained by having thousands of people around me who didn't know me or my situation. I was elated to finally be out of the public school system and to be treated more like an adult, for a change. When I enrolled at Sir George Williams, I chose to take a Psychology major in a Bachelor of Arts program – courses intended to help me understand the workings of my own mind. The same year that I registered at university, Marc began his first year of high school. Steven, who completed his last year at McGill and was now working, started teaching an evening course in September to first-year economics students at Sir George.

Because my brothers and I were all so busy with our own lives, there was rarely any time left over for us to spend together in the house anymore. However, after being in university for a few months, an incident occurred that brought Steven and I together again. I became a cheerleader for the university basketball team and had befriended one of the players, a handsome, black chap who was only a casual friend. One evening, Ross and I went to an after-game party. The house was jammed with people and as a result was hot and stuffy. It was raining and we couldn't go outside, so we managed to find an empty bedroom where we could catch a breath of air and talk alone for a while.

A few days after this party, my brother Steven was in the lobby of the Hall Building at Sir George when someone recounted an incident to him about "that girl," the one standing at the other end of the lobby – me – and about how she had been dragged out of a bedroom a few times during "that evening," the evening of the party. The girl who was gossiping about me didn't know that Steven was my brother, and according to the rumours, I had apparently been carrying on with several of the basketball players.

Later on that day after we had all eaten supper, Steven said that he wanted to talk to me and asked me to go for a drive with him. Even though he was sympathetic, something that was completely out of character for him when it came to me, I found the story that he repeated to me really horrifying. I remember our talk as if it had happened yesterday, because it had been so long since Steven had shown me any attention, let alone any understanding and compassion. After he told me about the rumour, he explained some things to me about university life. He said that it was like a city of young people, most of whom would never mean anything to me. He also said that the only people who counted in life were family and true friends, and that "real" friends would be above gossip and always try to help a friend in trouble. I was touched by this caring gesture, and his advice proved to be invaluable to me in future situations of social difficulty. However, we, as siblings, never applied these principles of wisdom with one another, nor could I ever count on Steven's support again.

When I finally made a few new acquaintances at university and started going out again, I was busy from morning until night. My father often drove me to school when I had early-morning classes. However, because we began to fight viciously in the car, I often got out at a stop-light and took a bus the rest of the way. It seemed that the more independent any of us became, the more agitated my father was. For the first time, even I found his company almost unbearable.

After I took all the mandatory, undesirable courses in my first year at university, in my second year I was able to study material that interested me and therefore begin my personal quest for peace of mind and self-understanding. I buried myself in literature: American, Greek, French, German, and English. I read countless books on child, criminal, and adult psychology which were required for my university major. I also delved into books about Hindu, Oriental, and European philosophy, as well as books on astrology and karma, especially rein-carnation. Although they weren't a replacement for an active social life, through these writings I was learning about other people's feel-ings and beliefs, which started me on my long path to recovery.

In these first two years at university, I made no close friends and had no lovers. I became fearful of relationships – of girls who wanted to be friends, and of boys who couldn't be only friends. I still couldn't shake off my grief long enough to believe that I could relate meaning-fully to anyone.

During this long interval, when I spent far too much time alone, thoughts of Mathew permeated every corner of my mind. When I read my books, listened to music, saw blonde boys, heard the daily sports broadcasts on the radio, and even when I ate good food, I was reminded of Mathew. Whether I wanted him to be or not, he was always there, for he occupied a private world in the deepest part of my soul.

Although his memory gave me great joy, most of the time it caused me an immense sadness. I even considered trying hypnosis to expel my obsessive thoughts of Mathew, but decided against it. In my mind, hypnosis made possible the idea of losing part of him, and that idea was unbearable because I missed him so much. It was a tragic time in my life, a time when I normally would have been free-wheeling and carefree, or perhaps trying to plan a career.

For the following two years, while Marc was making his way through high school, Steven and I were very busy with all our different activities. It was also during these years that many personal changes took place between the three of us.

After seeing what working for someone else had done to my father, Steven swore that his goals were to be self-employed and to become a millionaire by the time he reached thirty. He always loved flash and pomp, and because he always associated money with prestige and success, he was going to have it all.

However, due to this obsessive attitude, he surrounded himself with an impenetrable wall to keep out everything that was foreign to his goals. Expressing overt love and consideration became more and more difficult for him. Involvement with any other women besides his mother, his girlfriends, and, eventually, his fiancée was not possible for him, which counted me out completely. After that incident in the car, except for the occasional times when he wanted to meet one of my girlfriends, Steven and I never talked lovingly to one another again. What had previously been only childish arguments, now turned into a real hostility that created an incredible rift between us.

Although I was always thrilled with his accomplishments, he never appreciated any compliment I gave him. My opinion meant nothing to him as I was only his sister. I, of course, never accepted his rejections gracefully. I thought that after having been struck with the tragedy of losing a brother, Steven and I would appreciate one another more, but I was wrong, and time would prove just how wrong. Steven seemed to admire little more than my looks, and, in general, he made me feel as if I was not worthy of his valuable time.

Steven had just entered the job market and begun what he referred to as his "first ten-year plan to conquer the world." He busied himself with a full-time schedule of work and socializing, but as soon as he began working, he became particularly detached from the rest of the family. and under his seemingly happy and confident exterior, lay an anger that he controlled most of the time. I believe his stress over Mathew's accidental death caused great disappointments for Steven, disappointments that he never counted on experiencing. He had elected himself as an adult in the house ever since the time of Mathew's death, and his anxiety about my mother's deteriorating condition was clearly visible, as were his totally unfounded feelings of guilt about Mathew's demise.

Steven had always shown signs of economic genius and had studied business management at university. Because he had suffered so much personal pressure, he failed his last year. It was an unbelievable personal blow to his pride, but even worse than this was the fact that my parents never spoke about it.

When Steven began working, he wandered from job to job, a pattern that worried and agitated both my parents. Steven's undaunted confidence and determination to find work that would enable him to reach his goals kept him going forward, and I admired his ability to overcome my parents' negative input.

Because my father's attitude was demoralizing for a young man just starting out, Steven stayed away from him whenever he could. When they arrived at loggerheads, especially over the work issues, the rage they both displayed was frightening. Although the fact that Steven still lived at home was a financial advantage for him, his staying there became a nightmare. However, the nightmare only lasted two years, for Steven finally moved out of the house when he was twenty-three.

Unfortunately he took his rage with him, a rage that expressed itself over the years in two ways; one was a technique of his own, and the other mirrored my father's methods. In the first method, he provoked anger in other people by letting them act it out for him; in the second, he took on a know-it-all attitude that intimidated everyone. By continually mocking and criticizing them, his victims were left emotionally helpless, something he was especially adept at with me. Worst of all was the store of suppressed rage he harboured that maintained that wall he put up between himself and others, which made his methods more vicious when exercised. This served him well in business and with strangers, because there was no emotional attachment involved, but it almost completely estranged Steven and I as siblings.

Marc was the only one in the family who was really abandoned completely; my parents were working, he no longer had Steven for company, and I was busy with university life. Because Marc was the only child with a regular schedule, he was home most days at about three-thirty in the afternoon. Although he would play with friends occasionally or do his homework, he was very often alone and at age thirteen he basically became an only child. He continued to spend most of his time engrossed in all kinds of reading material and making things, as he had done with Mathew when he was younger. His reading material now ranged from mystery novels to newspapers, *Popular Mechanics*, and *MAD Magazine*. His favourite hobbies were making and disassembling model cars and airplanes, as well as building fantastic structures with his meccano set. Although these hobbies were very time consuming, he worked on them alone in his room, which was positive from a growth standpoint, but negative from a social standpoint. While engaged in all these activities, he usually turned the volume of his TV or radio up too high, which aggravated everyone, particularly my father. This was, I believe, Marc's way of expressing some of his anger towards all of us.

Marc had always been very independent, but at the same time he was also withdrawn and intense. My father continued to abuse him verbally, and although my mother usually rescued him, as she had always done, Marc was developing an anger towards my father that was even worse than Steven's. Although the rest of us were kind to him, no one ever asked Marc how he felt about being alone so much of the time, and he never offered to tell us. However, I now realize that he couldn't have known how to start talking about anything of a sensitive nature, for he certainly hadn't learned how to do so from the rest of us. When I moved out of the house, Marc ended up by himself completely. However, within one year of my leaving, Marc left home as well and rented an apartment with three of his friends.

Will and I were to be married in July. Marc had already informed my parents that he would be moving out the following year at the latest. Therefore, it wouldn't be long before my brother and I would both leave home. Although it had always been our belief that our father didn't really want us around all that much, the knowledge that all of his children would soon to be absent caused him to fall into what would be the first of several deep depressions, but the one that was to be the longest and the most severe.

Marc was preparing to move out of the house and into an old flat that was just a stone's throw from McGill. Under normal circumstances, having all of your children move out within a three-year period would have been distressful for the parents of any family, but in my parents case it was traumatic. My father was losing his outlet for expressing his frustrations about his uncle's treatment of him at work, an outlet he unknowingly was completely dependent on. During the last five years, my mother had deluded herself into thinking that she was working towards some sort of normalcy, but now she had to contend with the impending knowledge that soon all of her children would no longer be living at home with her. In addition, I now realize how apprehensive my parents must have been about not having the security of knowing where we were and if we were alright. Even more than this, both my parents were being forced to deal with loss again. Although it didn't occur to me at the time, I'm sure that the memory of having lost Mathew must have resurfaced, when, for so long, because of our physical presence in the house, they had been able to avoid it.

It all proved to be too much for Dad to cope with and he retreated deep inside of himself and became completely unmotivated. All of his joie de vivre and humour were no longer visible. He was quiet and confused. My mother found it almost unbearable having to watch him constantly. It was as if she was living with a complete stranger. On the advice of a psychiatrist, Mom took him for shock treatments. These outings were extremely tedious, for after he received the first treatment, he didn't want to go back. He also refused to return to work, but the psychiatrist told my mother that if he stayed home, he would regress even further into himself and could become suicidal, so she forced him to go.

My brothers and I felt very sympathetic towards my mother during this ordeal, but I felt even worse for my father. Even though I had studied about depression while in university, I was not prepared to witness a member of my family suffer through it. Marc, who was working hard at his studies, said that he was glad it was quiet in the house. His anger towards my father had reached a level which hindered his capacity for compassion. I remember telling Marc that I would have preferred Dad's aggressive and erratic behavior over his present condition any day. He completely disagreed, adding that he didn't want to talk about it any further and that, frankly, he didn't care.

I, on the other hand, continued to feel terribly sympathetic towards my father. I remember an incident that happened between the two of us before I moved out. My father was lying on the couch in the living-room, and as I was walking towards the kitchen, he called me to come over to him. I knelt down beside him and heard him say in a barely audible voice, without even looking at me, "Laura, do you love me?" I responded, "Yes, Dad, I do love you." He said, "Laura, tell me again." So I repeated, "Yes, Dad, I love you." I was so moved that I started to cry, for I couldn't remember when we had ever exchanged these words before. It was the first time that he had openly confirmed his need for my love. Normally, he was so angry and defensive that he was incapable of expressing such feelings. I was never able to talk to him about this incident, as I felt it might embarrass him, and it would be years before I would hear him say anything like that to me again.

I could hardly believe what was happening to my family. Steven had left the house in a rage only two years earlier, and now Marc was counting the days until he too would leave the house, also in a state of rage. My mother was never the same person after Mathew's death, and my father was in a deep depression. I couldn't wait to get away from all of them, especially my parents. My mother and father hadn't helped me through any of the problems of my youth, and I felt a general sense of abandonment and loneliness. I was about to fail my final year at school, and after that I couldn't cope with any more of their disappointment with me. I was furious at their continued expectations of excellence and performance on the part of their children, without their giving any tangible help, but I wasn't at all aware of just how angry I really was. That awareness was to come later, long after I left Will.

Once I finally had Will out of my life, my parents offered to let me stay with them until I could get back on my own feet, but only a couple of days after I was living back home, they made it clear that I should apply for unemployment insurance immediately, as well as begin looking for a job. This made me feel like both a financial burden and an unwelcome guest in their house. I found work selling office furniture, a job I hated and that I was completely unsuited for. I had to do something to keep busy and to avoid the disappointed eyes of my parents, who expected me to carry on as if nothing had happened. I also enrolled immediately in an evening course at Sir George, so that I could get my long- overdue and much-desired degree. I chose anthropology, which I took three nights a week. I found it fascinating and ultimately succeeded in passing the exam in September. I had returned home in May and would graduate in December.

I wrote my exam at the end of the summer and received the news in the fall that I had passed the course and would be graduating in the early winter. I recall that moment of success as being the proudest I experienced in years. My parents and the rest of the immediate family were very excited.

Steven and his girlfriend, Sandra, weren't able to attend my ceremony, and my parents had booked a trip to Florida during the summer in order to take advantage of a special rate. Because my parents' trip was arranged well in advance of their knowing about my graduation date, they told me that they couldn't come for this reason. Marc, however, was thrilled for me, and assured me that he would be delighted to attend.

I never expressed to my parents the extent of my disappointment at their not attending, as well as their not being willing to change their plans. I never forgave or forgot their insensitivity. It was just another confirmation of the lack of importance of my accomplishments, and

I vowed to myself that I would never count on them again, but I always held a special regard for Marc's support and his sincere joy about my success. If he hadn't been in the audience, I would have attended my university graduation ceremony alone.

Having been out on my own for over a year and a half, I found it unbearable living back at home. I was under my parents' constant surveillance, and living there now was worse than when I had left because I was alone with them. Marc left the apartment he had been sharing with friends, and was now living with a girl that my parents completely disapproved of. Steven was living with a woman named Sandra who was legally separated from her husband, and who had a six year old boy whom she was fighting to gain custody of. After having suffered a nervous breakdown due to her failed marriage, Sandra asked her husband to care for Kevin while she recovered in the country with her parents, during which time her husband had cruelly succeeded in having the court award him the boy. He accused Sandra of being an unfit mother on the grounds that she had abandoned Kevin. My parents only knew a few of these details and were horrified, but despite my parents' objections to their relationship, Steven remained with Sandra.

While I was working in furniture sales, I met a man who owned a group of new apartment buildings in Cote St.Luc. On one of our dates, I explained how difficult it was living back at home. He offered me a studio apartment at a preferred rate, and even though I knew that he expected certain favours for it, I gratefully accepted the studio and told my parents that I was leaving. As soon as I moved out, I quit my job in furniture sales and began searching for a new job. Unfortunately, it took much longer than I had expected to find work, and pretty soon I was broke. Being too proud and too ashamed to ask anyone to help me out financially, I was able to ward off my landlord with tears and excuses. On the days when I wasn't pounding the streets looking for a job, I never answered my phone at the apartment for fear it was someone who would discover the truth about my plight. The only time I ate well in that two-month period was when I visited my parents, which was about once a week, or when someone took me out for supper, which luckily was often enough.

During this time, I was having a relationship with Ira, an old friend of Will's who had his eye on me for years. He had the ability to really make me laugh, but despite his friendship and humour, the stress of trying to cover up my financial situation finally made me ill. I came down with bronchial pneumonia which made me extremely frail, and I was also anemic from weeks of having eaten so badly. Although I was so sick, I managed to keep all of this from my parents and my brothers, because I was afraid of their reactions. The two people who cared for me during my three week recuperation period were the two men in my life who originally wanted me only as a sexual partner. My landlord, Max, came and spent hours "babysitting" me and just talked, never once making an advance of any sort. Ira, who came to see me almost every night, brought me food and was delightful company. Neither of them ever judged me or asked me what my plans for the future were. They just wanted to see me well, as the illness and my problems had made me very depressed. It was because of the compassion of these two men that I eventually got back on my feet. They gave me more moral support in a few short months than any immediate member of my family had given me in years.

Regardless of my feelings of inadequacy, I always had enough confidence to call or approach anyone for work. I knew how to use my charm to get to see people, particularly men. A friend of mine who worked in a personnel agency told me about an opening in Public Relations with an advertising company called Clarke Billboards. He gave me the name of the General Manager, and even though he warned me that this executive had a reputation as a womanizer, he urged me to try and secure an interview, as he was sure I was perfect for the job. After unsuccessfully trying to reach this man several times on the phone, one day I presented myself at his office "dressed-to-kill," my waist length auburn hair tied back, but purposely left unbraided. I informed the receptionist that I was a personal friend of the manager and insisted on seeing him. She was aware of his reputation and promptly sent me up. He was so amused by my tactic that he hired me on the spot. As I needed the work badly, I convinced myself that I would find a way in the future to avoid his advances. The job temporarily dissolved my financial problems and my depression, and gave me the opportunity to meet Dianne who was to become, and still is, one of my closest friends.

The position at Clarke suited me perfectly. I was acquiring a new skill, and, because the job included a car, I had no trouble commuting to work. In addition, Dianne was there to help me learn about the company and to offer ways to ward off the advances of my boss. She was also someone to spend my lunch-hours with and to talk to. If it weren't for Dianne, I would have felt completely isolated in Montreal, as all my friends were either in Toronto or Vancouver.

7

ANDREW

Shortly after I started to work at Clarke Billboards, I met Andrew, who was introduced to me by his sister, Dee, who was visiting me from Toronto. Dee had been an invaluable friend during my marriage to Will, as well as my alibi on the evenings that I had spent with Caro. One night, while I was having dinner with my parents, she dropped in by surprise. Her brother, Andrew, was waiting for her in the car and he ended up joining us.

My first impression of Andrew was not a positive one. He was ugly, painfully quiet, and quite rough around the edges. When he did speak, he sounded like a gangster in a movie from the nineteen-thirties. He spent most of the evening drinking. After that initial outing, I didn't think about him or have any contact with him for several weeks. One day he got in touch with me and asked if he could see me. I agreed because I was lonely, and for our first date we went to a coffee house and just talked for hours.

Andrew's background was a type I knew nothing about. Even his sister Dee hadn't told me about their past, probably because she knew that I would feel either pity or disgust for it all. His mother was French Canadian and his father was Italian. They were poor lower-class and both were alcoholics. Andrew had been raised in the slums of Montreal. He had one younger brother who was married and living in Montreal, and his sister Dee was the youngest child. Dee was my age, and Andrew was nine years older than her. When Andrew and his siblings were very young, his mother and father were judged as being unfit parents; subsequently, the children spent years in various foster homes, which were only slightly better than the one they had come from. By the time Andrew was fourteen years old, he was out on his own and was involved in all kinds of criminal activities. By eighteen, he was locked up for months in a juvenile detention facility because of dealings in counterfeit money. After he turned twenty-one, he managed to stay out of prison, primarily because he was well practiced in not being caught.

The shady downtown areas and back streets of east-end Montreal, all of which were slum districts, were familiar territory for him. Because he was an alcoholic, he was also familiar with every club, bar, and speak-easy in these parts of the city. When we met, he was involved in some sort of illegal venture, but after we started to see one another seriously, he changed his line of work and began selling cars from an apartment building. This was a front for auto dealers who were pretending to be residents selling their own cars. Although I didn't like what he was involved in, he made a great deal of money at it, and, because I was already falling in love with him, I accepted it.

I never introduced Andrew to my friends and he never met my family. He was just too outrageous and I knew everyone would be horrified by him. This caused Andrew a lot of grief, for he insisted that I was ashamed of him. And although I continuously denied it, deep down inside I knew that I was.

So our relationship was clandestine. We spent hours alone together talking and confiding in one another about our past experiences. By listening to each other speak about the despair that we had both endured in our lives, we developed a mutual sympathy and understanding. He was surprisingly tender, patient, and compassionate; and by letting me act out and voice what lay hidden in the darkest corners of myself, for the first time since Mathew's death I felt the greatest sense of release from my deep-rooted grief.

Despite his lack of education and social advantage, he was quite well-read and therefore intellectually stimulating. He had an incredible sense of humour and a wild and adventurous nature. Most importantly, he was sensitive and basically unselfish when it came to me. He was also an unbelievable lover. He would always tell me that I was his "precious jewel," and he made me feel like the most beautiful and most desirable woman on earth.

The only thing I disliked intensely about Andrew was his drinking binges, which occurred about one evening a week. He was sloppy and weepy on these evenings, and, of course, irresponsible while drinking. He would spend large sums of money and always came home drunk. It was on these nights that we argued about everything, but I overlooked these binges because the rest of the time I spent with him was so enjoyable.

After we had been living together for about four months, he said that he couldn't continue with the "apartment operation" and that his options in Montreal had run out. He told me that he had been given an excellent offer to work at a used-car dealership in Vancouver, and that he knew the city well because he had lived there in the past. He added that it was a positive and honest step for him and that he was doing it all for me.

Andrew wanted me to join him out west. Finally, after much deliberation, I promised to follow him within a month, so he went on ahead of me. I was very worried about what I was going to tell my family, but I knew I wanted to be with Andrew. Besides, I was being sexually harassed by my boss at work to a degree that was unbearable, so I quit my position with Clarke and decided I would take a chance and go to Vancouver. I told my parents that I had a new job offer there and rehearsed this lie so well that I almost believed it myself. I had a friend in university whom I had kept in contact with over the years. She had a sister living in Vancouver, who I told my parents had helped me secure a job. I sublet my apartment, packed my belongings, arranged for them to be shipped, and left in August. I was now twenty-four years old and was strangely relieved to be getting away from Montreal and my roots again.

I wasn't disappointed with my decision. I found Vancouver to be like a dream-city. It was nestled in between a few of the Rocky Mountain ranges and along the Pacific Ocean. The landscape was breathtaking and the people were very friendly. In Vancouver, Andrew and I continued our irresponsible, childlike existence like two blissful teen-agers. Andrew changed the dealerships he worked for frequently, and because of this we lived in several different apartments. I worked occasionally, but mainly collected unemployment insurance.

Andrew did everything he could to make me happy. He bought me a lovely sports car and he also bought me a horse, a beautiful wild palomino that we spent many hilarious hours trying to learn how to ride, but never could. We purchased a twenty-foot cabin-cruiser in which we explored all the city shorelines, harbours, and Gulf Islands. Boating was our greatest passion, and the times we spent on the cabin-cruiser are among the happiest memories I have.

During the eighteen-month period that I lived in Vancouver, I buried myself in books, as I had while attending university. But unlike the years when I read for obsessive distraction, this time it was simply for pleasure. I read books on nature, vegetable and flower gardening, trees, photography, boating, horses, fish and other sea-life, and birds. I also read books about spiritualism, reincarnation, and philosophy. The two books that influenced my thinking the most were The Prophet by Kahlil Gibran, and The Tao Tse Ching by Lao Tsu. From the words of these two great writers I was able to find some peace of mind and understanding regarding my past and present existence.

This period that I spent with Andrew gave me back the chance to start accepting and loving myself again. It had been seven long and lonely years since Mathew's death, and I desperately needed to feel happy again. It was while I was in Vancouver that I began to remember Mathew with joy for having had him in my life for the time that I did, however short that was, instead of only remembering him with sorrow because I had lost him.

In spite of all this, I was unable to commit myself to Andrew. He wanted to get married and I knew I would never do that. Regardless of the freedom, the laughter, and the great love he gave me, I was shackled by my upbringing and the knowledge that he was not what I wanted, even though I wasn't at all clear on the kind of man I hoped for. I missed my friends, and, much to my surprise, I also missed my family. The family represented stability for me, and although I always felt uneasy around my parents and my brothers, I knew deep down inside that they loved me. Marc had visited me a few months after I arrived in Vancouver, and after he left, I started to pine for home. Andrew sensed my unsettled state and became desperate about it, for he couldn't stand sharing me with anyone else. He started to drink more and we began to argue a great deal. During these excessive binges he became verbally abusive, and I found this intolerable. We broke up a couple of times over his drinking, but because he caused such scenes at the homes of the people that I was staying with, I would go back to him after a week or two on his express promise that he would stop drinking, which of course never materialized.

Our bliss was turning into misery. I became afraid of Andrew, and one day I just packed up my clothes and left. The landlord in my apartment building sent the rest of my belongings after me by train. I called my parents from Toronto to tell them that I was coming home and that I would be arriving in a matter of hours, and they were at the airport waiting for me. It was November nineteenth, and I had been in Vancouver for sixteen months. For the first time in years, I was overjoyed to see my mother and my father. I was also thankful for their support, considering what a trauma it had been for them having me live so far from home for so long.

The day after I arrived home, my father suffered a massive gall-bladder attack. He lay in bed writhing in pain, insisting that it would pass and that we shouldn't phone the hospital. Despite his objections, I convinced my mother to call an ambulance, and we spent the rest of that evening waiting to hear that Dad was out of critical condition. His doctor informed us that his gall-bladder would have to be removed, as well as several stones that had lodged themselves in his pancreas, and that he would have died if we hadn't brought him to the hospital that night. However, to complicate matters, due to the severity of his attack, the doctor added that he would have to wait at least a few weeks in order to recover from the effects before he could be operated on.

My father had been informed five years earlier that he should have his gall-bladder removed, but he hadn't taken the diagnosis seriously. I found it synchronistic that I had come home just in the nick of time to help my parents through this ordeal and to provide company for my mother at home. As usual, she asked me little about what had transpired between Andrew and me, but for once I was grateful because I didn't want to discuss our separation with her, for I was convinced she could never be of any help anyway.

Now that I was living back at home, I knew that my mother would be frantic if I didn't secure a job as soon as possible. It didn't matter what it was I might have wanted to do, as long as I was doing something. I noticed that I wasn't as offended by their attitude to the degree that I had been in the past. I was beginning to understand my parents' debilities and was therefore becoming stronger, even when under their negative influence.

Steven worked successfully at a large personnel agency in Montreal, and, based on his performance there, I was subsequently hired as a Personnel Agent. The owner of Draker Inc. was a woman whom I admired and respected and who wanted nothing from me except good work. I had no pressures of the type I had in the past, except that I was on commission, but even that didn't bother me. I was working with a large group of women, the job was stimulating, and I enjoyed it especially because I was so good at it. Being a personnel agent also acquainted me with most of the important companies in the city, as well as what their products were and what their financial status was. This proved to be very useful to me later on, and I could see why Steven had used this form of employment as a training ground to his becoming a stock broker. By the time he had left Draker, Steven knew a great deal about the corporate structure of many businesses, and had worked with a substantial number of people who held top positions whom he could later contact as potential clients when he started out on his own.

Shortly after arriving home, I also resumed my friendship with Dianne. I really needed companionship and she was invaluable in helping me deal with my separation from Andrew. He had found out where I was working and called me three or four times a day for several weeks. Within two months, the receptionists all recognized his voice, and, as a result, only let through one call a day for the following four months until finally, after I told him that his harassment was putting my job in jeopardy, he stopped phoning. However, he continued to call me at home every evening, which so distressed me that, after several weeks of withstanding this, I took the phone off the hook when I went to bed and only put it back on in the morning.

It was a trying time for me because even though I had decided I could no longer live with him, I still missed him very much. I tried to concentrate on my work, spent many evenings with Dianne, and visited my father frequently during his six-week stay in the hospital. However, once Dad was home again and settled, I sensed I would soon have to move out. He still couldn't share my mother with anyone else, demanded all of her attention, and was particularly difficult and unpleasant while recovering from his illness.

Ever since my university years, I had dreamt of taking a prolonged trip to Europe. It was a humanities course which had covered ancient Greece and Italy that had convinced me to go in the first place, and I had spoken a great deal to Andrew about this dream. He had always encouraged me to try and realize it someday, and now Dianne took his place as the encouraging force in my desire to travel.

I gathered the pertinent material necessary to acquaint myself with all the countries I planned to visit, including: Scotland, England, France, Spain, Greece, Yugoslavia, and Italy. As soon as I started to work at Draker, I saved every penny. In addition, Dianne and I even started making toy frogs and promoted them to people that we knew in different companies. Everyone wanted one or more, and we found ourselves working most weekends trying to fill the orders for our stuffed frogs. It was the extra money I made from the sale of these toys that really made it possible for me to take my trip, and there was even enough money left over for me to rent a car instead of having to travel on a Eurail pass. The most marvelous news I received was in February, five months before my planned departure date.

Dianne was just coming out of a long-standing love affair, and she decided that the only way she could recover from this heart-break was to put some distance between herself and Montreal for a while. She managed to arrange a six month's leave-of-absence by signing a statement promising to resume her position with the firm after she returned, and by agreeing that before she left she would train someone to take over her duties. I was faced with a completely different set of circumstances. I decided not to notify my employer about my trip until one month before leaving, so that I wouldn't risk losing my job before then. I hoped that upon my return they might consider rehiring me. I wasn't going to let anything upset my plans, for this was going to be the first thing I had ever done purely for myself.

My next big hurdle was telling my parents. I knew they would have to adjust to the idea of my going to Europe, so, unlike my employer, I told them five months in advance. Their reaction was as negative as I could have expected it to be. I received a tirade of criticisms regarding my clandestine affairs, which they knew almost nothing about, my having lived in two cities over a period of only four years, and my having had five or six different jobs during that time. They held the opinion that I wasn't even close to wanting to settle down, and this made me an immoral, irresponsible, and unbalanced person in their eyes.

They ranted on about the fact that I had not translated any of my talents into dollars and that I was not in any way utilizing my education to attain some "wonder job." It never occurred to them that I left home because of a desperate need to get away from them and to try to find some peace of mind. They never understood that my relationships with men were a normal effort at trying to find love, or that I thought of my artistic talents as gifts to myself and others, rather than tools for money-making ventures. Furthermore, they also never took the time to realize that social work, the career that interested me the most, required several more years of university, and I was not presently prepared at this stage of my life to do that. My education had preserved my sanity in a way, but I saw it primarily as a privilege that I had been given, a huge personal asset rather than the basis for a career. My parents just didn't see any of it my way, which was one of the major reasons I always felt so alone while in their company. The fact that I was still "young and beautiful," which meant to them that I could still catch the eye of any man, was my only chance at attaining what they considered a normal life, and this reasoning of theirs really infuriated me.

Nothing they said could dissuade me from leaving for Europe. The only detail of my trip that they were relieved about was that Dianne would be joining me. Once they got used to the idea, even they became excited about my impending adventure, for at least in their minds they knew exactly where and why I was going.

I had one other satisfying experience before I left on this trip. Andrew came to Montreal to visit me after spending several months trying to convince me to see him. Our reunion was a painful but resolute one, because I found out that Andrew was finally out of my system. We spent an evening together making love and reminiscing about old times, but we both realized that the old magic was gone. Although we parted in tears, I was relieved to be free of him so that I could enjoy my trip with a clear conscience. He even gave me his blessings for the voyage.

8

MY TRIP TO EUROPE

Before I knew it, the month of July arrived. Only eight months had passed since I returned home from Vancouver, and here I was leaving again. I already earned the label of "the irresponsible, unconventional one," and was the greatest source of worry for my parents because I wasn't doing anything that showed them any promise for a solid future. They tried to have me contract their fears and limited way of thinking by telling me that I would end up alone and financially insecure. I understood that their struggle in dealing with Mathew's death had left them emotionally crippled, and that seeing one of their children venture so far away from them must have been terribly stressful for them. They, however, never tried to see my point of view, even after I tried to clarify all the measures Dianne and I had taken to ensure our safety. The only member of my family who didn't think the idea was crazy was Marc, as he and Alice were planning to take a year's trip to Europe and Africa after they graduated from architectural school, before settling down to work.

When the plane finally lifted off, I experienced an enormous sense of release and joy; however, my feelings were also tinged with sadness, for at that same moment I became aware that living at my parent's home made me feel imprisoned and somewhat depressed. Soon, I overcame my melancholy feelings, because our new adventure began immediately on the plane. Dianne and I met a couple who were living in Glasgow, our first destination, and who invited us to stay with them while we were in their city. They were a Canadian couple who were on diplomatic service in Scotland for two years. Because Dianne and I were slightly nervous, we were delighted with their invitation. Jan and Beth were exactly what the doctor ordered, and their hospitality gave us the confidence we needed to move on without any fear.

Dianne and I journeyed through Scotland and England by bus, where we met all kinds of charming people who were also travelling. The British were very receptive to the fact that we were Canadians. This warm reception occurred in every country we visited, which made the entire trip so much more pleasurable.

After three weeks, Dianne and I set off from Dover for France to begin a four-month experience that we would always remember in vivid detail. We picked up a little Renault Four in Paris, and proceeded on a four-thousand mile trip that took us through the back roads of France, Italy, Greece, Yugoslavia, and Spain. We encountered more interesting people on those roads than we did for the following ten years of our lives. I couldn't believe the hospitality we were received with from complete strangers in all of those countries.

We both saw an endless array of natural and man-made wonders, ranging from the azure coastlines of Yugoslavia to the magnificent Swiss Alps, the ruins of the Parthenon in Greece and of Pompeii in Italy, Michelangelo's sculptures in France and Italy, and even Marco Polo's house in Venice. The whole trip was so emotionally and intellectually fulfilling that it gave me more satisfaction than any other travel experience I was to ever have in future years. Through it all Dianne proved to be the perfect travel mate, because our extraordinarily different personalities complimented one another and made the holiday all the more entertaining. I never thought I could enjoy myself with someone as much as I did with Dianne, and, to this day, we still reminisce and laugh hysterically about our experiences there.

While we were travelling, I kept a diary of what we did and how I felt. I also asked many of the people we met to write little excerpts into the journal as keepsakes. Two of the most memorable passages were as follows: "Be not forgetful to entertain strangers for thereby some have entertained angels unawares," Hebrews XIII: 2 and a quotation from G. Crabbe, a fourteenth century English poet, who wrote: "Life is not measured by the time that we live." The first excerpt made me realize that it was possible to be affectionate with, and well received by, complete strangers, to like them more than members of one's own family, and not feel terribly guilty about that. The second excerpt gave me special comfort for the first time concerning how I always suffered due to the brevity of Mathew's life. Somehow it made me feel that the quality of his existence, as well as the love he had been able to impart to those around him in the limited time he had with us, was so great that I gained some relief from this thought. Mathew, of course, was on my mind always, but, once again, as when I was in Vancouver with Andrew, I was able to remember him with some happiness.

Dianne and I reluctantly returned home in December of that year, heavy-laden with keepsakes and gifts from every country we visited. We had declined all kinds of work offers and romantic possibilities. To this day, I sometimes regret these lost chances to further travel and develop myself.

Both sets of parents greeted us at the airport with open arms. They had vicariously experienced the trip right alongside us, the parts we wanted them to know about, due to the large number of letters we sent them while we were travelling. In the final analysis, I think they were thrilled that we had the opportunity for such a wonderful adventure.

I stayed at my parent's home for several months until I found myself a downtown apartment. I had been accepted back at Draker as a personnel consultant based on my past performance. For the first time in years, I felt stable and really confident about myself, and for the first time since Mathew's death, I was back in Montreal because I wanted to be.

Marc and Alice were busy planning their impending trip to Europe which was only six months away. Steven had purchased a Burger-King restaurant at the beginning of that year, and was on the verge of negotiating the purchase of a second one. He had quit Baiche & Co. about eight months before I left for my trip to Europe, and, with the fortune he had made in the stock-market, decided to go into the franchise "fast-food" business. As was the case with everything he tried commercially, it was working out splendidly.

Marc and Alice were pleased for Steven, but for the moment all they cared about was gathering as much information as I could give them about my trip to Europe, as their projected travel itinerary was to be an extended version of my trip. Steven, on the other hand, still considered the entire affair an extravagant self-indulgence on my part and, frankly, wasn't really concerned about anyone's activities except his own. He was thirty years old now and was obsessed with becoming a millionaire before he reached the age of thirty-five – some sort of elevated goal he felt he had to achieve in order to show everyone how brilliant he was. Of course, this meant he had to work almost continuously in order to achieve this goal, and, therefore, spent little, if any, time with his children. Kevin was now eleven, and his hostility towards Steven was beginning to manifest. Ronnie, who was two years old, looked upon Kevin as his role-model, brother, and friend. Sandra accepted Ronnie's and Kevin's relationship, and was also turning to Kevin as a sort of friend.

I was very worried over this unbalanced family social structure, but was too involved in my own difficulties to try and help anyone with theirs. I also surmised Sandra had enough problems without my attempting to offer any psycho-analysis about the status of the members of her household. I hardly saw her anyway because she had accepted Steven's unspoken condition that if we were to become friends she would inadvertently be betraying him. I hoped that, with time, Steven's attitude would change, but I knew it would be far into the future if it ever did change at all.

9

THE RIFT CAUSED BY MY ABSENCE

Before I go on with my story, I feel I must elaborate on Steven and Marc's lives in Montreal during my two and a half year absence in Vancouver and Europe. Steven and Marc never left Montreal during this period. They were now twenty-eight and twenty years old, respectively. Marc was still in university because, after having spent three years in engineering, he had decided to change his faculty to architecture. This meant it would be another two years before he would graduate. At this stage in his life, my parents perceived Marc as a professional student who didn't know what he wanted to do, but because he had been living away from them for so long, he was able to ignore their attitude. He was still sharing an apartment with Joyce, who came from one of Montreal's very wealthy "establishment" families. Although neither sets of parents approved of their association, their relationship lasted for a couple of years until insurmountable problems between Marc and Joyce finally split them up.

Marc was devastated over their separation. I remember how much I longed to try to comfort him, but I realized that due to our family's long-term silence, I too was becoming unable to help my family member's, even if I wanted to. The memory of how I felt watching Marc walk aimlessly around the house after Mathew's death came back with a frightening clarity, as well as how helpless and guilty I felt about not being able to relieve his suffering.

Marc never really got over Joyce. Her lively spirit had given some of the joy back to him that he lost when Mathew died. Now he was back inside himself, even more withdrawn than before, and concentrated most of his efforts and time into his studies. He managed to get through this period with the emotional support of Scott, a close friend that he made in university who was also studying architecture, and it was through Scott that Marc eventually met Alice.

Alice came from a Hungarian family and she had only one brother. She was also studying to be an architect, and because her home was in Toronto, she was living in residence at the university. Marc and Alice started out as casual friends, but their friendship flourished into a serious romance. Alice was beautiful, young, and Jewish, so my parents were delighted. Marc and Alice had many things in common and within a short time they were making plans together for the future.

On the other hand, Steven and Sandra had married just before I left Will. It had been a lovely, tastefully-done wedding, with only immediate family and close friends attending. Although my parents started off with endless objections to Steven's being with Sandra, she was so charming they couldn't help but love her. In order not to have my parents interfere with their lives, Steven told them little about their personal problems. What really surprised my parents was that Sandra converted to Judaism, which she insisted was as much for her as it was for Steven. However, once she married Steven, all I ever heard about her was through the reflection of my brother and his activities.

As I have already mentioned, Steven and Sandra were awarded custody of Kevin, so, after a couple of years of only weekend visits, they now had a little seven-year-old boy living with them who was completely traumatized and scarred from his experiences. Steven was twenty-eight when Kevin started to live with him and Sandra. My brother, who was training to be a stock-broker at the time, had no room in his life for a troubled child. After Tom disappeared with Kevin, Steven hired a lawyer and a detective who eventually found out Tom's whereabouts, and, because Sandra got her son back through

Steven's dedicated efforts, she accepted his complete disinterest in her son. She took it upon herself to support her husband's career at any cost, and convinced herself that, with time, Steven and Kevin would develop a closer relationship.

Sandra allowed Tom to visit Kevin occasionally, and Kevin maintained his father's family name. Although Steven and I never spoke about it, I thought that this must have been very difficult for him. Right from the beginning our family all saw that Steven wasn't capable of being any kind of a positive father figure to Kevin. He was intolerant and insensitive towards him, and although he gave the boy everything he wanted materially, he wasn't able to give him his love. Because I found it unbearable to observe the way Steven treated Kevin, I became even more distant from my brother than ever before.

I loved Kevin from the beginning of his inclusion in our family. He was a beautiful blonde boy who reminded me of Mathew, and, although I also found it disturbing that he was born only five days before Mathew had been killed, the major reason I saw Steven and Sandra was because of him. Visiting with them made me realize how my father's attitude towards my brothers when they were young had affected Steven's disposition towards his own child. He treated Kevin exactly the same way Dad had treated him as a boy.

Although Steven's boyhood situation was completely different than Kevin's – Dad hadn't really started to mistreat Steven until he was about ten years old – everyone in my family just accepted his behavior, which made me resent them all the more. For the first time, I felt as if I was beginning to despise Steven, and I couldn't comprehend Sandra's seemingly despondent acceptance of his conduct.

When Ronnie was born, he was an absolute "hit" with my parents because he was their first grandchild. Thank goodness that Kevin had been the first grandchild born to Sandra's parents and that they truly adored him, otherwise I don't think that Kevin would have survived the secondary place he withstood after Ronnie was born. But time would prove that Steven would not be a much more tolerant parent with Ronnie than he was with Kevin.

When I returned from Vancouver, Kevin was ten years old, and Ronnie was almost one and a half. Ronnie's presence brought the family together, socially, more often. Because I had been away from Montreal for such a long period, I felt disconnected from all of them. I asked my mother for as much information as she could give me regarding Steven's and Marc's activities since my absence, for I was sincerely interested. I discussed some of my Vancouver experiences with my sister-in-law, Sandra, and with Alice, but I could never manage to see either one of them alone, as my brothers were always around. I hoped that they repeated portions of what I told them to my brothers, but, even if they did, there was never any feed-back from either Steven or Marc.

Somehow my absence had created a huge rift between my brothers and I, but I couldn't understand why. They both seemed despondent towards me, or, more often, they were aggressive and angry – especially Steven. It was as though my having moved away was some sort of unpardonable sin. I was aware that my parents had used them as an audience to voice their criticisms and fears about my unconventional life-style; however, I hadn't expected that Steven and Marc would adopt my parents' attitudes. This surprised me, particularly because I thought my brothers would be sensitive enough to realize how fortunate they both were to be settled with mates, and that I needed their support because I was alone. But I was sorely disappointed. Marc and I still held some affection for one another, but Steven and I remained distant. The only reason I stayed in contact with Steven was because I had a desire and a need to see his children.

My family occasionally drove to Steven and Sandra's house for Sunday brunch or for supper. I found these outings more and more stressful as time went by. Steven treated me with contempt, always making some insulting or critical remark, which provoked me into a hysterical state. I tried to dismiss the idea that only someone for whom a person cared about could get under one's skin the way Steven got under mine. I wanted his affection, if not some simple respect and courtesy, but I never received any.

The tension in Steven and Sandra's home resembled my family's during our childhood, but Steven had taken my father's place as the instigator of discord. He brought our dysfunctional family profile right into his own home, with the exception of an additional weapon which he used against everyone that Dad had never had; Steven had wealth. He was basically rude and arrogant to everybody, but he was the most condescending towards me. One afternoon at his home, after a particularly ugly scene had transpired between us, I appealed to Sandra to talk to Steven, but after speaking with her I realized that he might never change. She explained to me that although I believed that because my brothers and I had lost a sibling we should cherish one another all the more, in actuality, Mathew's death had the opposite effect on Steven; he closed himself off emotionally from almost everyone. She said that even she rarely had the opportunity to share his innermost feelings.

Sandra's revelation regarding Steven's closed emotional state distressed me terribly. In addition, my anguish over Mathew's death was being revived because of the constant rejections I was receiving from both my brothers. This period of my life marked the time when I started grieving for Mathew in a way that I had been able to avoid for years, and this made me feel even more alienated from my family because I couldn't share any of these feelings with any one of them.

The first year of his marriage, Steven started working at Baiche & Co. However, before he began, the company sent him to New York City for a few months to train for the job while Sandra remained in Montreal to care for Kevin and Ronnie by herself. My brother had now been in the field for a couple of years and was doing brilliantly. Although he was a workaholic, and, for the sake of his career, saw little of his children or his wife, my parents found his lifestyle acceptable, if not admirable. He purchased a spectacular house in one of the poshest areas of the city, bought several cars, and collected paintings, antiques, and anything else that would be considered an investment acquisition.

Steven's ever-growing income and subsequent possessions provided Sandra's parents and my own with endless conversation about
his accomplishments. I often wondered how Marc felt hearing this
continuous account. I was concerned about his feelings of self-esteem
regarding his still imminent career and how well he would do, but we
never discussed it. I had one brief exchange about this with Alice after she confirmed having the same worries as me, but we never found
the time to talk about it either.

My parents continued to extoll Steven's business genius whenever
the opportunity arose, which eventually made my mother and father
appear as superficial as Steven was becoming. However, they never
spoke of his patronizing attitude towards everyone, of how, because
money represented superiority to him, he used his wealth to express
his aggression on all the people around him. None of us seemed to
warrant his precious time, and nobody was intelligent enough to have
the privilege of conversing with him. Because everyone was in awe
of his success, Steven was able to vent some of his bottled-up rage by
simply negating most things we said. It was as if he decided that, for
every moment that he had suffered over the years, the people in his
life would have to somehow pay, especially loved ones. He wasn't even
aware of how obnoxiously he was behaving. My mother overlooked
much of Steven's offensive demeanor, even when he treated my father
with increasing disrespect and contempt. Because I had been gone
long enough, I was able to focus on just how irrational my family was,
which made me feel like an outsider. I was thankful for Kevin and
Ronnie for giving me the sense that I somehow still belonged.

When I took a closer look, I also noticed how my parents were
taking all their children's personal problems to heart. They seemed
truly offended by our individual dilemmas, and offered little sympathy and no empathy at all. Our lives had not turned out the way they
hoped or, rather, expected they would have. Furthermore, my mother and father never considered our problems as being unique to the
times, which were very fast-paced and transient, which compounded
how stressful these problems were for all of us to cope with. They

married very young, and therefore couldn't understand our "love-affairs," divorces, and work instability.

Neither one of them ever worked for anyone else except family, and so they didn't understand the enormous competition out in the work force, but my mother understood to a certain degree once she returned to work at the age of forty. Their general opinion was that we were unstable and lazy. Regarding our personal heart-breaks, both my parents, and my mother in particular, believed that nothing my brothers and I experienced was traumatic compared to having lost a child, and therefore we could never know suffering equal to hers. She never said this, but we knew she thought this way, and, although theoretically this was true, I felt she had no right to use Mathew's death as a measure of the depth of our own personal failures. After all, we too had lost Mathew, but, as always, that didn't seem to count.

10

RAINER

During the year that I was employed at Draker, I met a man who worked for the executive male placement section of the company. He made some very discreet advances towards me the first few weeks I was back on the job, and finally got the courage to ask me out on a date. I had just broken off from a short-term romance with a temperamental artist, and I needed someone whom I could simply feel comfortable with.

Rainer was born in England, and even though he had been living in Canada for over twenty years, he still retained a charming British accent. Although he had originally trained to be an engineer, after practicing in the field for several years, he decided that the profession didn't appeal to him, and chose instead to place engineers in positions with different companies. Both his parents were deceased and he was an only child. He had lost his entire family in the Second World War, and had chosen to come to Canada when he was in his twenties, and he never left.

For about a ten-year period before we met, Rainer had had a long affair with a married woman. She had three children, the youngest of whom was Rainer's son. This was a well well-kept secret that I suspected during our entire affair, and which I found out to be true towards the end of our relationship. Even though he was no longer seeing the mother, he frequently saw the boy, whom he insisted was his protégé.

Rainer had all of the conventionality, good breeding, education, and fine comportment that all of my previous partners lacked. Almost twenty years my senior, he had been a world class soccer player for England, and therefore had a fine, youthful appearance like a man in his mid-thirties.

A lone and quiet individual, with a combined air of sadness and wisdom about him, particularly to someone my age, Rainer had no ties of any kind, as his best friends had all been transferred to other cities, so the most attractive thing about him was that he needed me so much. I had his undivided attention, first because I was so much younger than he was – something that really appealed to him – and second, I was the right social class and had the right amount of education. As the weeks passed, I found him to be stimulating, energetic, thoroughly pleasant, and a truly sympathetic listener; and, after a short but intensive courtship, we moved in together.

An added positive factor going for Rainer was that I had a family that I could share with him. And he was the first man that I was proud enough of to present to them all. Although they thought he was too old for me, they were enchanted by him and delighted with the way he treated me. Despite the fact that Rainer was aware of my family's troubled interpersonal relationships, when I was with him, it was bearable to be among them. Rainer brought peace into my life, something I never had with any other man I lived with. I was also relaxed in his presence.

The artist whom I had a brief affair with just prior to living with Rainer was a playboy, and, unfortunately, only a few months after Rainer and I had begun cohabitating in my studio apartment, Rainer developed a serious infection that was diagnosed as a case of gonorrhea. He had in fact contracted this condition from me! (This illusive venereal disease is carried benignly by a woman, but makes a man extremely sick.) We both were required to take penicillin, which cured us in ten days. As soon as I was well, I got in touch with my former lover John and informed him that I had reported him to the city's venereal disease control center, and denounced him for what an irresponsible man I thought he was for not having informed me that he had this disease before I had a chance to pass it on to someone else. The unfortunate result of all of this was that Rainer was old fashioned and was therefore appalled by the entire episode. Our sex-life was never quite the same, but, quite frankly, I didn't really care too much at the time. I had so much trouble with men sexually in the past that I was pleased that Rainer was attracted to me for more than just physical reasons. So, despite this pitfall, we remained together.

After we had been going out for close to a year, Rainer and I decided to find and share a large apartment together. He was rarely at his own place, and my "bachelor" was really too small for a couple. We found a beautiful apartment in one of the older sections of the city, where we lived for a couple of years. Because we also worked for the same company, we made a point of seeing other people for lunch.

We were really active socially due to all of Rainer's varied interests. He patiently tried to teach me how to golf and bowl. I enjoyed the latter, and we belonged to a bowling league that posed as our social club. I met his two best friends through the league, and found them to be terrific people whom I became close to during our four-year affair. We shared many enjoyable activities with Mary and Lance, including vacationing in Florida with them each winter.

Because he loved to go camping, Rainer lured me out of doors a great deal. He was utterly fascinated by the fact that Andrew and I had camped out in the Rockies with nothing more than a pup-tent, a couple of sleeping bags, and our fishing rods. Our expeditions were just as private, but not quite as primitive as those in B.C. Our favourite place was a camping area at Saranac Lake in New York, where we reserved a small island and motored out by boat with all our gear. We had many hilarious outings there, as we were particularly unlucky with the weather. I remember numerous occasions when we tried to sustain a campfire by standing over it with an umbrella in the pouring rain.

About two years after we met, I left the personnel agency and found a job as the Promotion Director for the most elegant underground shopping mall in the city, which was owned by one of the largest real-estate companies in Canada. I secured that position through the vice-president of the company, who had recommended me despite my lack of experience in that field.

A short while after I began working at Chrysler Inc., I noticed that Rainer started to drink, which was very unusual because he was so health conscious. Within a couple of months, he came home one day and told me that he was no good for me, that he was much too old for me, and that he felt we should therefore split up. He added that his job at the agency was going nowhere and that he was thinking of quitting. I was absolutely knocked flat by all of this. I couldn't bear the idea of his leaving me, as I was so content with him and didn't want to be alone, so I pleaded with him to stay.

Although living with Rainer was not what my family had envisioned as an ideal existence for me, while we did live together, I could visit them and not feel completely out of place, the way I had always felt in the past. Marc and Alice lived in Toronto, but came to Montreal often to visit. Rainer and I made a habit of getting together at my parent's home with Marc and Alice, or more often at Steven and Sandra's, which gave me a chance to have contact with my family, especially the children who were the ones I really wanted to see. I was distressed about the way I was using Rainer as a vehicle to see my family in a comfortable setting, but I couldn't help how insecure I was. I even tried to convince myself that I really loved him, but, of course, I knew that this wasn't true. I just hoped everything would stay the way it was, but that was impossible. Matters became progressively worse after that, and one day he announced to me that he had been investigating a job offer in Personnel down in Florida, and that he planned to take the position. He also expected me to accompany him.

I couldn't believe I was hearing this from my conservative Rainer. His words sounded like a ghost from the past, for he was proposing the same upheaval that Andrew had proposed not more than five years earlier. I screamed that we had leased an apartment together which I couldn't afford on my own, that I also had a job with incredible opportunities for future advancement, and that it appeared he was deliberately sabotaging all of that. Of course he denied this completely, and I was so naive at the time that I wasn't able to clearly see what was really happening. So, like a fool, I gave up our apartment and my job in order to join Rainer on his "fantasy" adventure.

He left a month before I did, and called every couple of days to tell me how beautiful the weather was, how friendly the people were, and how much he liked the office. But when I finally arrived there, I discovered to my horror that he had not researched the American work and immigration laws to the extent that he should have, and we ran into all kinds of problems in being able to work there legally. Again, I couldn't believe it! I had resigned from my wonderful job and left our apartment for this man, and here I was back at point zero. But fortunately, the last few months of the year that I spent in Florida, I managed to find someone who let me work under-the-table. During those months, Rainer stayed at home, resigned to his depression due to his phenomenal blunder. I was beginning to see that I would soon have to leave him, as I had lost all respect for him. Even Mary and Lance, his two closest friends, gave up on him when they found out about this situation.

Rainer and I were sharing a cottage with a friend named Tom, whom we had met while living in our first lovely beach house those first few months in Florida. He was a croupier who worked in the large casino in Freeport for about a year, and was now taking some time off just to bum around. He proved to be an invaluable friend to me. As much as he liked Rainer, he strongly encouraged me to break up with him. With his support, I finally mustered up the courage and made all the arrangements in secret. It was only two days before I left that Rainer found out about my plans.

Tom drove me to the airport with Rainer hot on our tail. The scene that he made there was horrible. I ran through the departure gate while Tom held Rainer back physically. Rainer was crying and screamed that he would not survive without me and that he would kill himself if I left. It was like a nightmare, but, as soon as the plane was airborne, I once again felt as if the weight of the world had been lifted from my shoulders. I never wanted to see Rainer again. At that moment I suddenly became aware of how often in my life I had run away from people, and it began to worry me.

11

HOME TO STAY

I was now thirty-one years old and was returning to Montreal to stay, though I didn't realize this at the time. Convinced that the family would give up on me completely at this point, I didn't know whether or not I would be able to bear their scorn, as even I was disgusted with my state of affairs. I had no real career to speak of, no place of my own to live in, no savings in the bank and no prospects for a relationship. I wasn't even depressed about all of this, I was just plain angry. I was angry with myself and my family, but I was particularly furious with men. I decided that I had to thoroughly examine what had happened to me these last ten years, so I could continue with some sort of positive outlook. And because I felt I had nowhere else to go, I was back at my parent's home. My old friends Claudine and Dermit offered to let me move in with them, but I didn't want to interfere with their lives to that degree.

My parents were as upset and disappointed with my situation as I expected them to be. They were unsympathetic regarding my dilemma and seemed reluctant to find out what had happened in Florida, which I also expected. My father, however, was disappointed because he had sincerely liked Rainer. I explained to him that Rainer and I had a sexual problem in that he had become somewhat impotent. I didn't reveal how this actually came about, but told him instead that our difficulties had evolved over a long period of time. Although my father was satisfied with my explanation and felt it sufficient reason for our break-up, we also talked about another problem, which was Rainer's mid-life crisis. Dad was able to shed some light on this subject for me as Rainer was only twelve years younger than he was. But after this brief exchange, we never spoke again about these topics. Quite frankly, I was overwhelmed that Dad had discussed these matters with me at all because we had never talked about such personal issues before, and I was truly grateful for his input.

What really caught me off guard was my mother's malice. She expressed real fear about the possibilities for my future, as if my time left for a "normal" life was running out. I remember one afternoon in particular, just a few days after I arrived home. She lost control of herself and said many dreadful things to me. She told me that I was reckless and irresponsible and that, considering how many men I had slept with at this point, my reputation was ruined to a degree that most men would now perceive me as some sort of "whore." She defiantly added that when she was my age she already had a home, had given birth to two children, and was pregnant with a third. She also expressed her disgust about my not having established any kind of career along the way, and that she and Dad were sick of bailing me out of my escapades. I was totally shocked by her unexpected verbal attack. I felt as if I had now lost the support of the only person in my immediate family circle whom I thought I could rely on for acceptance.

I raced out of the house and jumped into the Camaro that Rainer loaned me to use until I got myself a job. I drove wildly around our neighbourhood, feeling like a frenzied, trapped animal. I went through stop signs and red lights, never thinking for a moment that I might kill someone, as I didn't even care about myself. But some force protected me, and after fifteen minutes of this "recklessness," I found myself back in front of our home, exhausted and full of loathing and resentment for my mother. I stormed into the house and shrieked that I would never forgive her for the things she had said to me and that I would be "out of her hair" as soon as I possibly could. The way I felt towards her changed that day, and I didn't forgive her until many years later. I'm sure she sensed my change in attitude towards her, but, of course, she knew she had everyone else in the family in her corner. I was accustomed to having no one in mine, but was used to occasionally having her there.

I didn't want to be with my family or anyone else for that matter. Because I had spent my last few months in Florida relatively confined with Rainer, I needed the anonymous crowds of downtown where I could lose myself, yet still feel like I had lots of company. This need for anonymity was a replay of how I felt when I entered university and needed the anonymity of the crowds there to numb my grief over Mathew. I was thinking about him a great deal again. Unfortunately, whenever I was with my family and felt their general lack of support and interest in me, I longed for his unconditional affection.

I particularly wanted nothing to do with men. Looking back on the last ten years, I remembered how many of my employers had hired me primarily because they wanted to go to bed with me. All of my love affairs had begun with sexual advances. It seemed as though from the age of sixteen on that most males had only approached me based on my looks and not because of the kind of person I was. Neither my father, nor my mother, nor my brother Steven had ever offered me any advice about this common problem that women face, but then they had seldom helped me deal with any problems, except for that one incident with Steven when I was in university. My mother never even spoke to me about these things or how to deal with them, except on one occasion, when she told me always to have enough savings in the bank so that if an employer made an inappropriate advance, I could quit my job without being worried about my financial position. If she had only known how frequently this happened to me, then she would have been overwhelmed by how sizeable a savings I would have needed.

I decided that the man of my dreams, even a compromised version, did not exist. I told myself that I would find an attractive, rich man who wouldn't be too concerned about the fact that I didn't adore him as long as I fulfilled his superficial needs. At least I would be well off and settled in a thoroughly acceptable arrangement, in everyone else's eyes. I told myself that I wouldn't have any children, because I never wanted to love anyone as much as I felt I would love a child. Besides, I only wanted to have a child with a man I loved deeply, and I was convinced that was not going to happen. I believed that if my heart was broken any more than it already had been as a result of Mathew's death, I simply wouldn't want to go on living.

So I occupied myself visiting with the only friends that I cared to see. Claudine and Dermit continuously tried to convince me to live with them, which I foolishly refused to do. I saw Dianne frequently, too, as she and her fiancé, Frantz, lived only ten minutes from my parents' house. I also took strolls on the mountain, went to movies, and, when they were the most crowded, walked alone through the streets and malls of downtown Montreal. I often engaged in these activities after unsuccessfully searching for a job all day.

While at home, I read voraciously to fill up my nights, so that I wouldn't have to spend more time than was necessary with my parents, as I felt like a burden to them. I was beginning to feel despondent towards Marc and Alice because they expressed little interest in me, and I saw Steven and Sandra only occasionally in order to continue to keep in contact with their children, whom, as usual, I considered to be the only pleasant and sane people in our family. Steven was as contemptuous as ever, and Sandra never once asked to see me alone so that she could talk to me and perhaps help me out with my upset family relationships. However, I didn't resent her as much as I felt sorry for her because I was aware of how Steven had complete control over her, and I suspected he prevented her from getting close to me.

Ever since I'd come home, Rainer kept pursuing me in the same manner that Andrew had after we had broken up. He called repeatedly and finally flew up to see me. Claudine and Dermit offered us their house for a day so we could be alone. I knew that our affair was permanently over, but Rainer's visit convinced him of this as well, so he returned to Florida to stay. Later on that year, I learned through

Marg and Lance that he had spent five months in a sanatorium, after which time he married a girl twenty-years younger than he was, and eventually found a job working as a landscaper. I hoped that someday he would be content, despite what had happened between us.

I began spending much more time with Dianne and Frantz. Dianne provided a compassionate ear by letting me speak endlessly about the previous ten years of my life and how I felt I had ruined those years. I based my negative deductions on the fact that neither as a child nor as an adult, had I ever experienced a nurturing relationship with a male, except with my brother Mathew. I became aware as I spoke to her that I had in fact unconsciously orchestrated the failure of all my love affairs. I experienced so much rejection from the male members of my family that, due the fears created by this, I had become terrified of any real emotional intimacy with a man, as that would eventually become a serious love relationship, and the possible loss of that love was too unbearable a risk. My affairs had been based on very normal needs; however, I had chosen men who needed and loved me much more than I needed and loved them. They all had serious character flaws that I knew would eventually make me want to leave them, and therefore I knew in advance that I had a valid reason to get out when that time came. This defense mechanism was an assurance that someday if they withdrew their love from me, I would easily survive because I had never really committed to them in my heart.

I remembered Rainer had once tried to tell me these things, but I wouldn't listen. He explained that because my only great love relationship with a male had been with my brother Mathew, my expectations of how a man should love me were distorted. After all, Mathew had been my brother, and I was looking for a mate. He added that although Mathew and I had a perfect kind of affinity for one another, I couldn't possibly expect such built in acceptance and compatibility with a stranger at the beginning of an affair. I was amazed and horrified by Rainer's accurate analysis. Suddenly I knew I had to change the way I thought about my relationships with men, but I didn't really know how I was going to accomplish this. But I felt that my new re-alization would give me a better chance in the future. I further be-lieved that after all the different jobs I worked at, cities I lived in, and fascinating people I met, I could now clearly and maturely get on with my life. I thought about how lucky Steven and Marc were to be settled down, and I longed for the stability and the happiness that they both seemed to have found with their partners. I decided that I would like to, and possibly could, have these things as well. These thoughts proved that I was experiencing some hope for the first time in a long while.

On one of the evenings that I walked over to Dianne and Frantz's house, I met Edward, an old friend of theirs who was staying at their place two nights a week. I found it peculiar that I had not arrived on one of the evenings that Edward was there before this, or that Dianne and Frantz had never mentioned this arrangement to me. Edward had been separated from his wife for about eighteen months, and was living up north in a half-built house that he was working on in his spare time. He left his wife the apartment they shared in the city, and had moved out to the only place that he wouldn't have to pay rent. However, as he found commuting very difficult to get used to, Dianne and Frantz offered to share their place with him until he got used to the commute. He worked as an independent sales agent representing several different companies that manufactured window coverings, such as drapes and blinds. He was well established with his customers in Montreal, and had no wish to change his line of work or his territory. Dianne and Frantz also supported Edward emotionally while he was recovering from the trauma of his failed marriage.

The way I met Edward was very comfortable and somewhat old-fashioned in its chaperoned nature. I found him to be thoroughly charming and extremely handsome. He had black hair and green eyes with long, thick, dark eyelashes – an attribute I found irresistible. He was thirty-five years old, of medium height, and had a lean build – the kind of body that any sort of clothing looks wonderful on. Very soft-spoken and polite, he had the manner of a well raised European.

I discovered that he loved fine wine, classical music, jazz, and books – mainly non-fiction. He wasn't interested in spectator sports, nor did he like involving himself in activities with other men, but preferred instead to engage in singular activities like swimming, bicycling, cross-country skiing, and walking. The most attractive thing about him was how un-North American he was, despite the fact that he had already spent half his life in Canada by the time I met him.

After that first evening, I thought nothing more of our meeting, for I was still committed to not becoming involved with any man. When I went to see Dianne again the following week, Edward was there. This time we retreated to the balcony where we talked for hours. He told me that he had been married for over six years and that he had a two-year-old daughter. Which parent was to gain custody of Pamela had not been settled yet, so she was staying in the home of their baby-sitter while Edward and his ex-wife alternated taking her to their respective homes on weekends. Edward was very careful to downplay the topic of Pamela on this particular evening, and spent most of the night recounting some amusing episodes of his travels with two friends across Canada and the States when he was in his early twenties. Sometime in the midst of this exchange, we were suddenly aware that both of us were struck with a whopping case of "lust at first," or rather, "second sight." It was such an intense attraction, and I was delighted because for the first time it was mutual.

12

LIFE WITH EDWARD

Edward and I spent our weekends together from that evening on. My parents were used to my passing a lot of time with Claudine and Dermit, and therefore didn't suspect anything when I told them that I was going with my friends to the Eastern Townships. In between these weekends together, Edward and I started seeing one another a couple of times a week, so my parents were finally able to meet him. My mother and father were both completely captivated by him and were especially impressed by his quiet, gracious, and well-bred manner. He was totally different from anyone else in our family, particularly the men, and Edward was the first man I dated whom my parents didn't find anything to criticize about.

I helped Edward find a winter tenant for his country house so that he could sublet a friend's apartment in the city for the season. That way, he avoided the stress of daily commuting, and we were with one another when we weren't working.

We spent most of our first month together either making love, eating out, going to movies, or taking walks. It was on these walks that we divulged our pasts to one another.

I was truly fascinated by Edward's experiences as we had really come from two different worlds. His mother was born and raised in Vienna, Austria and she had two younger sisters. His father, who was Dutch, had one older sister. Having graduated as an engineer in his early twenties, Mr. Van Dor had worked for five years in Holland for Shell Corp., before moving to Rumania.

However, after being employed in Bucharest for three years, he returned to Holland because he no longer wished to practice engineering, and he offered his services to the Dutch government. He was given the post of Ambassador to Holland in Bucharest, where he served for over ten years. During his third year in Rumania, Mr. Van Dor met Edward's mother. She was twenty-three at the time and was working as a nanny to three children of a Rumanian family. His parents fell in love, married, and had two children. Mrs. Van Dor, who was a great beauty, adapted very naturally to the aristocratic life that she and her husband enjoyed while living in Rumania. They entertained a great deal for the Embassy, and also attended other government parties and dinners. To facilitate matters, they hired servants including a cook, a maid, and a nanny for the children.

When Edward was nine years old, and his sister Barbara was six, Mr. Van Dor was notified that his post would soon be over in Rumania. The family was given the choice of being transferred to either Venezuela or Quebec. Mr. Van Dor, who was fluent in five languages, one of which was English, accepted the position of Consul in Montreal, as neither he nor his wife were prepared to go to South America. Although their children only spoke Rumanian, Dutch, and German fluently, they were able to get by in English due to a special effort Mr. Van Dor had made over the years to acquaint his children with the language by teaching them many words and short phrases.

Edward's family returned to Holland for a short stay and then left for Canada. Their lives changed drastically from that moment on. Edward told me that his mother never recovered from the transition back to an average life, especially in a strange country where she couldn't speak the language. In Montreal, the family lived in an ordinary duplex on an ordinary street. Mr. Van Dor had his job to occupy his days and was therefore very content, but Mrs. Van Dor felt alienated, because she didn't have any close friends or relatives in Canada. She couldn't seem to get over the shock of these changes, and as a result, became an angry and embittered woman especially after her children had grown up and her beauty waned.

Edward, on the other hand, was enthralled with his change of life-style. He had never been in a public school before, or been allowed away from his Embassy home while living in Bucharest. He always had private tutors for everything, from his schoolwork to golf lessons. Now he was "on the street" with a bunch of boys, trying to fit in. He told me that he had felt completely liberated, like a bird having been let out of a cage. Barbara was just starting school, and Edward's mother worked on the child's overly sensitive nature by over-protecting her, and finally debilitated her emotionally to the degree that Barbara was never able to leave her parents' home later in life.

Edward's family lived an un-rooted existence for years to come. Once his post was over in Montreal, Mr. Van Dor was sent back to Holland for just under a year while waiting to be assigned a new position as a Consul. This new job ended up being in Basel, Switzerland, where Edward and his sister went to the renowned Rudolph Steiner alternative school. They studied there for five years, until Mr. Van Dor was transferred to Germany for another five-year term. By the time this happened, Edward was in university, and his parents decided to let him stay in Switzerland to finish his studies. To this day, Edward speaks of the Swiss with contempt for their arrogance and how they made anyone from another country feel eternally like a visitor they had allowed in, no matter how long they resided in their country.

When Mr. Van Dor's post was completed in Germany, he finally retired. However, because Barbara secured a job as a lab technician in a hospital in Vienna, Edward's parents moved to Austria with her. Mrs. Van Dor, however, had no intention of giving up her "stronghold" on Barbara, so she ended up in her city of origin in order to be near her daughter.

Edward was thrilled to be on his own, and, while in university, met a couple of fellows that were to remain life-long friends. Although he frequently went to Aachen to visit his family, he remained unattached to them emotionally and didn't miss them during this period. Upon graduating, he planned to take a trip to Canada and the United States with two friends, with the intention of making New Zealand his final destination. He believed he would eventually return to Europe to live. He did travel to Canada and the States, but never made it to New Zealand because he didn't have the right kind of visa, which is how he ended up back in Montreal. On account of his decision to remain in Canada, Edward's mother never forgave her son, because she wanted him to return to Europe and live near her.

When Edward and I first became involved, I remember cooking supper together one night in the make-shift kitchen one night at the cottage. He announced to me that he was never going to get married again and leave himself vulnerable to so much heartache. I was already in love with him, so I jokingly said that I felt the same way, but we knew we were both lying. Within weeks, we were practically living together at his apartment. I managed to find a job at a radio station, in the promotion department, so I moved out of my parents' house and into my own place, but I spent most of my time at Edward's. We started to make plans for a future together, with Pamela as our major issue of importance.

Edward was the first person that I allowed myself to love unconditionally since Mathew had been killed. He was also the first man whom I ever considered as a permanent partner, which was still very painful for me to contemplate because I was always afraid that I would lose someone that I had decided to love so deeply.

Edward was particularly tender and patient with me, regarding my never-ending struggle to overcome my grief over Mathew, no matter what form it took, and I adored him for it. Edward's transient background had given him a strong desire to settle down and have a home of his own. During those first few months together, we had many memorable moments, and we soon decided that we would transform our "love-shack" up north into a home. The prospect of building a house really inspired me creatively, and I became totally committed to manifesting it into our "dream-home."

Edward and I were meant to be together. Although we differed from one another in many ways, we found a deep love that I still often marvel at. Compared to me, he was quiet, and emotionally withdrawn. By the time we met, he had been completely separated from his family for over twelve years, and after that trip to Europe with his first wife, his mother and sister had flown over only once to see Pamela, when she was a year old. Edward's involvement with my family was to be one of the hardest adjustments he experienced because he no longer understood that having immediate family close-by had a dramatic effect on one's life.

Edward habitually spent Wednesday evenings with Pamela. However, during our first month together, he saw her several evenings a week because he skipped a few of his weekend visits with her so that he and I could be alone. I met Pamela right at the beginning of my affair with Edward, when the three of us spent one of our weekends up north. She was two years and ten months old at the time, and was a sweet and intelligent child who instantly charmed me. The first time that she and I were alone together, we were sitting at the camp table in the dining room of the cottage, and as she scrutinized me, I sang one of Barbara Streisand's songs to her. Pamela was enchanted, and this "singing" became one of our traditions before bedtime for many years to come. But at this stage of our relationship, I wasn't ready to spend a lot of time with her alone, as I hadn't spent enough time with Edward yet.

I was amazed at how tortured Edward was over his legal status regarding Pamela. He also despised his ex-wife to a degree that alarmed me, and he had not yet finalized anything about Pamela's custody – or his divorce, for that matter. The only thing he had taken care of was the legal separation and his wife's financial settlement, which was more of an accomplishment than Edward realized. However, he considered it minor compared to the things that weren't yet reconciled. Apparently Edward's marriage had never lived up to his expectations. Like so many young women, his wife Louise was insecure, and although ready to leave home, she wanted to get married and have someone take care of her. Edward told me the story about their marriage during one of our long walks on Mount Royal. He began by saying that, like most over-rational thinkers, he concluded that after having secured a job and an apartment, he should get married.

He met Louise in a discotheque, found her to be attractive and interesting, and decided that she would be a fine mate. They lived together for eight months before Louise told Edward that she couldn't continue forever with their illicit living arrangement. He agreed to marry her despite the fact that he found her to be somewhat depressive and negative. She was also prone to illness and was slightly frail because she was so thin. He told me that he convinced himself that these flaws were minor and that they would improve with time, especially once they were settled down. At the time of their marriage, Edward was twenty-seven and Louise was twenty-four years old.

Although Louise was already well established as a teacher, Edward wasn't committed to any job. During their second year together, when she was offered the opportunity to teach in France for a year through a teacher-exchange program, they moved to Europe. While in Europe, they met Edward's parents who were living in Aachen, and they also travelled around central Europe before they started to work. Unfortunately, Edward's mother disliked Louise from the moment she set eyes on her, but I believe she would have disliked anyone whom she felt had taken her son away from her.

Life in Europe was very different and very romantic compared to life in Montreal. While Louise taught, Edward studied philosophy courses at the town college, as French Immigration informed him that he couldn't work; and on weekends, they travelled to other countries such as Germany, Italy, and Spain. At the end of that year, they returned to Montreal and started back into a normal life together, but their relationship began to deteriorate.

Louise's depressive temperament worsened and Edward wasn't the most understanding person at that time when it came to emotional issues. Just like Edward's mother, Louise was shocked by her "real-life" responsibilities, and when she became pregnant four years later, there was much discussion over whether or not she should have the child. In a final, but futile, attempt to save their marriage, they decided to keep the baby. Louise's negative nature was greatly compounded by the stress of a newborn child, and her post-partum depression lasted for over a year. It was during that year that their marriage fell apart. Edward had no comprehension or sympathy for his wife's apparent lack of joy over the birth of their child; moreover, he was exhausted from working all day at his job driving a taxi. He would spend half his evenings without sleep as a result of taking care of Pamela, while his wife, who had taken a year off for maternity leave, stayed in bed crying.

When Louise returned to work the following September, both agreed that their marriage was over, and by the time the New Year came along, they decided to split up. Pamela was sixteen months old at the time. Edward and Louise already managed to find a girl who lived only a block away to come in and babysit for Pamela during the day while they both worked. Pamela seemed to love Leanne, and Edward and Louise agreed to share the child-care expenses.

Shortly after Edward moved out in February, Louise began to harass him for all kinds of financial support that, in fact, she was not entitled to. Fortunately Edward found a lawyer who talked Louise's lawyer into accepting a settlement which was comprised of most of the belongings in the apartment they had shared together, plus a set sum of money. The most distressing situation for Edward was that Pamela was with a third party, which of course couldn't be helped. However, within one and a half months of their separation, Edward learned that Louise had been asking Leanne to keep Pamela with her overnight at least twice a week. By the time three months had gone by, Pamela was staying with Leanne an average of four nights a week. Louise also frequently reneged on her week-end visits, shortening them to one day, and sometimes less. Edward, on the other hand, was diligent about seeing Pamela every Wednesday evening and every second week-end, and sometimes he saw her more often due to Louise's negligence.

Until Edward and I had been seeing each other for a few months, I had not taken Pamela really seriously as a possible continuous person in our lives. Apparently, from the time that I first appeared on the scene, Pamela was talking about me incessantly to Leanne, who was delighted, and to Louise, who was horrified. As soon as she heard that the child was interested in someone who appeared to be becoming permanent in her ex-husband's life, Louise promptly renewed her interest in seeing Pamela. She also upset Leanne's schedule by taking the child against her will whenever she was in the mood, and told Pamela that I was only a "passing friend" of her father's. Leanne felt that this was not proper for a three year old to hear, and one day she gave Edward and me an ultimatum. She told us that she had been keeping a record of Edward's and Louise's conduct towards Pamela since she had first started taking care of her, and that if Edward didn't move to settle the custody in his favour, adding that Louise was incapable of taking care of a child, she would no longer be willing to keep Pamela.

I found myself faced with the biggest dilemma of my life. Edward and I had already started to speak of marriage, but had carefully avoided the issue of Pamela's future. At this point, I already loved the child as much as she loved me, but the prospect of having her full time hadn't occurred to me. I was really afraid of the responsibility and wasn't sure of what I wanted.

Edward was also trapped. He explained that he was torn between his responsibility and feelings of guilt regarding Pamela, and his desire and love for me. He explained to me that although he believed Louise would probably ruin the child's life if she had custody, he would give her the child if I didn't want Pamela to live with us, because he needed me more. The option he gave me, however, was that if Pamela had to be with Louise, he didn't ever want to have another child – not even with me. I argued that this ultimatum was pure black-mail on his part and that he was dumping his messed up past in my lap, but he refused to understand this and held his ground. I didn't know what to do. I was being pressured from all sides when everything was still so new. It turned out that Louise only wanted visitation rights. Leanne was constantly telling me how much the child loved me and how much she needed and deserved a family, and Edward was suddenly telling me that he had a duty towards his child and had to act on it. I really had no other choice, but I felt somehow betrayed by Edward for the way I was pushed into the situation.

We gained custody of Pamela only nine months after we had met. Louise agreed to visitation rights every second weekend and on certain holidays. At least that way Edward and I were assured of having some time alone, but I really had no idea of what I was getting myself into. Edward and I gained custody of Pamela through a simple and brief meeting in his lawyer's office.

Pamela had already been living with us for four months, during which time we brought her to Leanne's every morning then picked her up every night when we came home from work. When the legal proceedings were settled, Edward and I were still only engaged because his divorce had not yet been finalized. I found it unusual that the court granted us custody considering the fact that we were not yet married, but the arrangement seemed to suit everyone.

Leanne had given us her diary, the one profiling Edward's and Louise's conduct towards Pamela since the time Leanne had taken her into her care, to use during the negotiations in case Louise made any trouble for Edward in the course of the custody hearings. Lucky for us, initially, Louise didn't cause us any problems, so we put the diary away for future reference, should the need ever arise. Louise was quite satisfied to have visitation rights which she took advantage of only when it pleased her, which was every second weekend and on certain traditional holidays, such as Christmas and Easter.

Edward and I moved from our one-bedroom apartment into a two-bedroom in the same building. I proceeded to decorate an adorable room for Pamela while trying to get used to her continued presence in my life. I was working full time, but managed to take two weeks off so that I could spend some time with Edward and Pamela at our chalet up north. After that vacation, we made the difficult decision to tell Leanne that we were enrolling Pamela in a daycare center that was very close to our home. We explained to her that, because Pamela needed to integrate into this new environment, Leanne would not be able to see her for a few months. I remember that task as being one of the most arduous I have ever had to undertake, because Leanne was more of a mother to Pamela than any one had ever been. She was as distressed by this news as we had expected her to be. Although Louise seemed undisturbed by this new arrangement, she objected strongly to the choice of daycare center because it was an English one. She tried to legally stop us from enrolling Pamela, but was informed that she had no rights regarding the issue.

That legal stipulation began six years of court battles with Louise that almost succeeded in ruining Edward's and my marriage, as well as Pamela's stability and peaceful existence in a real home. Louise was sold on being one of those modern women who has a third party raise her child, and whimsically exercised her rights whenever it suited her; that way she felt she would never jeopardize her guise as "Mother." But even though Louise was her biological mother, she had cared for Pamela full time for only a year, and when I began to raise Pamela, she was bonded more to Leanne than she was to Louise. Then, shortly after Pamela started living with Edward and I, she began to accept me as her mother.

Louise was not prepared for the way Pamela and I bonded together, for she believed that I was just a passing fancy of Edward's. It only took Pamela two months before she was calling me "Mummy," and that initiated enormous trouble for all three of us. On the weekends that Louise took Pamela, she would tell her things no child of three could understand, which included details of her on-going affair with a married man who had children. Mainly, she instructed Pamela continuously that I was not her mother in any way, shape, or form, and that she shouldn't call me "Mother." When Pamela was with her, Louise bought her extravagant gifts, let her do as she pleased, and, in general, played the part of the devoted, over-indulgent parent. Pamela would return from these outings confused, exhausted, and emotionally upset, which caused Edward and me a great deal of despair, as we didn't really know how to cope with the situation, except to try to limit Louise's visitation rights. Louise also called Pamela twice a week, which she had never done when Leanne was caring for the child, and we often found Pamela very upset after these calls.

Louise's first attempt to place a strain on our future plans was to find a way to deny Edward a divorce, so it took an additional year before he received his final papers. For years afterwards, she dragged us in and out of court making all kinds of unreasonable demands that required no commitment on her part, but that she knew would put enormous strain on our three lives as we struggled to become a family. Leanne explained to me that Louise never imagined that Edward would find a serious partner, especially one who would become a parent to her child. It took six years, but we eventually eliminated Louise from our lives, and I discovered that I could love a child that was not biologically mine as much as I could love any blood relation – if not more.

From the beginning, I acted like the typically neurotic parent with their first child. I visited about ten daycare centers before deciding on the "right" one, when, in actuality, they were all about equal. I busied myself by sewing clothes for Pamela and produced an over-abundant casual and dressy wardrobe. I also shopped for books and toys and all sorts of paraphernalia all parents tell themselves their children need, which proved to be the most fun of all. However, I had to go on most of these shopping sprees alone because all of my closest friends were living in other cities, and neither my sisters-in-law, nor my mother offered to accompany me.

After work and on weekends, I spent as much quality time as I could with Pamela. I took her to the park behind our apartment building, played games with her, read to her, prepared meals with her, and, in general, immersed myself in the task of making this child mine. Edward was not as involved with Pamela as I was, and the strain of my responsibility began to show its effects early on. For instance, he was often critical about what I expected of Pamela. He would ask me what she had eaten during the course of the day, which I took offence to, first, because he knew how particular I was about her meals, and secondly, because while she had been in Leanne's care she was fed badly and he had done nothing about it.

As the years went by, I also discovered that Edward preferred to be with his daughter in small doses only, admitting that he found children to be tiresome and boring. Unlike my father, Edward was not critical or tense while he was with Pamela, and he did spend some quality time with her, especially when it came to doing sporty things like swimming, biking, and skiing.

I, in turn, expected far too much of Pamela almost right from the beginning. I found that I was often unjustly impatient with her, but, thank goodness, I had the presence of mind to be willing to explain my frailties to her, as well as to apologize –something my own parents had never been able to do. Like all new couples, Edward and I needed to spend time alone together, which we now seldom got, and that caused us a great deal of frustration.

Everyone in my family just sat by and watched the painful process I was going through, making me feel as if I was performing some sort of task that I should be able to carry out with excellence and with ease. I was finding out, however, that motherhood was not at all the elevated and natural state of affairs it had always been extolled to be. Instead, it was very stressful and was something one had to learn as one went along. Although I knew my mother had raised her four children practically on her own, I was hurt because she seldom asked me how I felt or how I was coping, and I believed that she and my father just expected me to be a "perfect" mother. Because I had never been pregnant, I never had any time to get used to having a child, nor did I receive any of the attention and support most women are given by their families and friends during that period. I was an instant wife and mother, and that took its toll on me.

That first year we were all living together Pamela contracted pneumonia four times. The last time she came down with it, the doctor warned us that her immune system had been badly damaged. He also said that if she caught pneumonia again she could possibly die. Subsequently, I became completely neurotic about everything she did for months after. I also found it difficult to work the first eight weeks that Pamela attended the daycare center. Because she didn't want to leave us, when we dropped her off she was carried in screaming and kicking every morning. Eventually, she loved the place and talked about it for years to come; but while she was getting used to it, I arrived at the ad agency in tears and couldn't concentrate for hours. As a result, I couldn't perform my job properly and eventually I lost it.

Edward and I were finally married in November, three months after I stopped working. We had a lovely, simple ceremony conducted by a female justice of the peace. Edward's parents flew in from Vienna, and my immediate family and a few close friends also attended. The reception, which was held at my parent's home two days later, was as delightful and entertaining as I always imagined it would be.

Ten days after we were married, Edward and I decided to move up north permanently. I saved six thousand dollars that year, and we paid off the one outstanding loan Edward had taken out on the house with his ex-father-in law's money. I felt as if we were being given a fresh start, and Edward promised that, if after a year I found it too isolated living up north, we would move back to the city. But I was excited about the prospect of this new adventure, and I was also pleased that Pamela would be further away from Louise.

Pamela didn't sleep through the night until she was about six years old. Especially after her visits with Louise, she had nightmares for several days and would wake up screaming, which exhausted both Edward and I. All of these problems, coupled with Louise's constant interference, put such a strain on our relationship that I often wondered whether we would make it or not. For the first time in my life, I understood why women stayed married for the sake of their children. I had grown to love Pamela so much that I couldn't bear the thought of her suffering on account of our possibly splitting up. I knew that if a separation did occur, I would lose her to Edward because I was not her biological mother. Strangely enough, a few years later I discovered that I would have had an excellent chance of winning Pamela in a custody battle with Edward, even though I was the adoptive parent. For the moment, I felt completely trapped.

I had great difficulty coping with my family's lack of empathy, as they viewed my position as an outsider who had taken someone else's child to raise. At times, I even lost my patience with Edward. He didn't understand the incredible strain I was going through due to Louise constantly telling me that Pamela wasn't mine, while, in actuality, I was feeling more and more like she was my own child with each passing day. He gave me the impression that I should just rise above the distress this was causing me. How unjust I thought our situation was, because at least in a legal adoption the biological parents have no rights to interfere with the life of the adopted child. The fact that Edward was a biological parent and I was not was the source of most of our problems. For years, Edward wouldn't admit what an incredible psychological advantage he had over me because of this, and it was only through a therapist, who gave him documentation on the topic, that he really became sensitized to my predicament. But we found a solution to this problem; we decided to try and have a baby together.

In April, six months after we moved to Morin Heights, I became pregnant. Pamela would now have the much-needed sibling she so desperately desired, and I would feel fulfilled as a woman. I didn't tell anyone that I was pregnant, preferring to keep this delicious secret to myself for a little while. I found myself spending many a blissful hour wondering how he or she would look. Would my child have Edward's spectacular green eyes or my mother's strawberry blonde hair? Would the hair be straight, curly, fine, or coarse? How long would it take him or her to sleep through the night? I also imagined tiny hands and tiny feet. I imagined singing lullabies, and cooking beside a radiant, gurgling infant who was rocking in a little chair. The thought of the two of us crawling around on the floor, playing baby games, or dancing together made me laugh to myself.

Because the baby was due in December, I also played with the notion that perhaps my child would be Mathew's spirit incarnate. When I was three and a half months pregnant, the normal amount of time considered to be out of risk of losing a baby, I made the announcement to my immediate family and a few close friends. Everyone was thrilled and I was the happiest I had ever been in my life.

13

MISCARRIAGE

B efore I had found out I was pregnant, Edward and I had planned a trip to Vancouver in July to visit Dianne and Frantz, and to share a sailing holiday with them. Pamela was to stay with Louise during our absence, which I tried not to be too upset over. I checked with my general practitioner to see if it was safe for me to fly, which he assured me it was; however he instructed me to sail only under the calmest of weather conditions. I had not visited my gynecologist since I became pregnant, but told myself I would do so when I returned.

The flight was comfortable and went smoothly. After spending a few days in Vancouver, visiting the sights and driving around admiring the spectacular scenery, we set sail for a ten-day cruise through the Gulf Islands. During the first two days of our trip, the weather was overcast but not turbulent, and on the third day it was clear and sunny. Dianne and Frantz's boat, the Mahalo, was a very stable and luxurious craft, and we all enjoyed being on the ocean, admiring the view, and taking pleasure in one another's company as well as Frantz's fine gourmet cooking.

In the evenings we moored up to a "log-boom" which was a huge collection of logs chained together, usually parked on the shore of an uninhabited island, waiting to be picked up by a tug-boat and brought to its ship for loading. We were moored at such a spot on our fourth night out and had retired to our individual bunks. In the middle of the night I experienced intense abdominal cramps and had to wake up Edward because I had to go to the bathroom and the side of the bed I slept on was against the wall of the cabin. It was awkward crawling over him, struggling to get out of this tight space, and we had to muffle our laughter so as not to awaken Dianne and Frantz. It was pitch dark, but I didn't want to turn on the light because the bathroom was right beside their cabin. I felt as if I had a bad case of indigestion, and yet I couldn't seem to go to the bathroom. The strange thing about it was that I also felt as if I had urinated for about five minutes. Nevertheless, I shrugged it off and went back to bed.

Within half an hour, I was again awakened by these cramps and returned to the bathroom. This time I turned on the light and read a magazine, determined to stay there until I got rid of my upset stomach. I had no success, except I again felt as if I was urinating for an abnormal length of time. I stood up, looked in the toilet bowl, and saw that it was full of blood! I began to panic. I returned to our cabin and asked Edward to move against the wall, in the event that I had to get up a third time. I explained to him about the blood, and he suggested that we motor in the morning to the nearest town clinic.

We never got back to sleep that evening. Within fifteen minutes, I returned to the bathroom for the fourth time with unbearable cramps that I began to realize were unlike anything I had ever experienced before. I was suffering from severe contractions and was losing a great deal of blood in large clots. I yelled out and woke Dianne up, because at this point I was really terrified. Edward had been sitting in the dining area just beside the bathroom for some time now keeping me company.

After spending twenty minutes in the bathroom with me, Dianne said she suspected I was having a miscarriage. Although I responded that this was impossible, I was bleeding profusely and did admit that I needed to see a doctor as soon as possible. My contractions were occurring in ten minute intervals, so I remained on the toilet while Edward tried to comfort me by holding my hands. Dianne and

Frantz released the boat from its moor and set out for the nearest large town. It was fortunate that they knew the waters well and were confident about their direction because it was the middle of the night. They radioed ahead and instructed the coast-guard to have a taxi standing by to take me to the hospital immediately upon our arrival. It took us about two hours to get there, but the cab was there waiting for us.

Dianne lined the back seat of the taxi with a plastic sheet, laid me down, and placed the contents of a half a box of Kleenex over my vaginal area, then covered me up with a blanket. Although she was trying desperately to calm me, we were both weeping. The taxi made its way to the hospital, which was about half an hour's drive. Edward and Frantz, who had remained at the marina to close up the boat, arrived at the hospital about twenty minutes after Dianne and me.

Two nurses immediately placed me on a rolling bed and whisked me off to the attending obstetrician. Edward walked in just as the doctor and his staff were explaining to me that I was indeed having a miscarriage. I felt as if I was losing my mind, and started screaming that it couldn't possibly be true. I was four and a half months pregnant and had been feeling perfectly healthy having taken especially good care of myself. I argued desperately that it simply had to be some complication which they would certainly remedy. The doctor tried as gently as possible to convince me that I was having a miscarriage and that he needed my cooperation to help him with the delivery.

I continued yelling and crying so bitterly that I think I alarmed the staff. Restraining me physically – as I was terrified by now and completely out of control – they administered a large dose of Demerol to knock me out in order to make things easier for all of us. Edward was crying and looking on helplessly as he witnessed this scene. I remember watching him stagger towards the wall, weeping and shaking his head saying, "I'm sorry baby. My poor darling, I'm so sorry." As I begged him to stay, a bleary-eyed nurse helped him out of the room. For a brief moment I had a flashback of my father seventeen years earlier, staggering into the hallway of our home on the evening the police came to inform us of Mathew's death, and I felt a shudder pass through my entire body.

I again told the doctor that I wasn't giving my baby up and that he'd have to find a way to save my child. Finally, after about six hours of my fighting the effects of the Demerol, I remember, just moments before I went under, hearing the doctor whisper that he had never been involved in performing such an arduous delivery in all his fifteen years of medical practice. Poor man! Even though I almost believed there was no hope of my baby's being alive, my closing words to the obstetrician were that I still didn't want to relinquish my child. In the late evening, I awoke to see the face of one of the nurses who announced that it was all over. Her words crushed me and I felt completely beaten. I realized at that moment that I had no emotional ability to deal with death. All I could think about was how my mother had lost Mathew, and for the first time I wondered how she had survived. I felt like dying and I had merely lost a half-term pregnancy.

I felt so empty, spiritless. I had a vision of my child extending an outstretched arm to me, and as I reached for him he slipped away into a distant light. As he faded from my sight, I was left in complete darkness, paralyzed with grief.

I had to remain in the hospital for one more day after I miscarried. The hospital lab technicians were going to autopsy the fetus and mail the report to both me and my doctor in Montreal. As it turned out, I was in the miniscule percentage of cases whose babies were genetically perfect, the knowledge of which only compounded the tragedy for me. The baby had become disconnected from my uterine wall and had died – it was that simple. The doctors had no idea why this had transpired, and a year later my doctor decided that I would require a cervical stitch to ensure that this would not occur again in the event of subsequent pregnancies. Unfortunately, this diagnosis was reached only after I had had another miscarriage.

Needless to say, our holiday was completely ruined. We all sailed back to Vancouver in a terrible funk. Edward and I spent an additional few days at Dianne and Frantz's apartment before flying back to Montreal. When we landed, I was still in a state of shock, and didn't yet realize the destructive, long-term effects this experience would have on me, as well as on Edward and Pamela.

Although everyone in the family expressed their condolences over my miscarriage, none of them came to stay with me. I found their behavior astoundingly thoughtless, even for members of my family. Their almost passive reactions made me even more aware of how damaged and emotionally crippled they really were. It was clear that none of them understood anything about my needs, including my own mother. My brothers didn't even call, except to send a message via their wives. And neither my sisters-in-law nor my mother perceived that I would have benefitted by the comfort of their arms around me. They also neglected to ask how I felt in the weeks following, believing that with time my pain would simply disappear, which of course it —didn't – just as when people stopped inquiring how we felt so soon after Mathew's death, my family's pain heightened. I was completely traumatized, and they were as silent as mutes, just as usual.

I was very listless those first few months after my miscarriage. Mostly, I felt completely alone and was resentful of Edward's and Pamela's blood-ties for the very first time. Although this resentment produced a sense of guilt, I couldn't help myself.

My miscarriage was the first in a series of events within the next year that really tested my desire to live. I wanted to become pregnant again right away. I found myself the finest fertility expert in the city, and he set up an appointment in December for Edward and me to undergo artificial insemination, even though we had been trying on our own for only four months. We were incredibly lucky, for I conceived after our first session. It was like a miracle!

Over the Christmas holidays, my brothers, their wives, and their children stayed with us for eight days. I was only five weeks pregnant at the time, but just after New Years' Day I noticed that I was spotting blood. I became panic-stricken and informed Sandra who had had several short-term miscarriages before giving birth to Kevin and Ronnie. She told me to see my doctor immediately in case it was something serious, but tried to reassure me by citing several examples of her friends who had spotted during their entire pregnancies and who had nevertheless delivered to full term.

I tried to feel confident after listening to her, but still experienced a sense of dread. Sure enough, ten days after our guests left, I was rushed to the hospital in the middle of the night where I succumbed to nature's demand on me – I had my second miscarriage. Afterwards, the shock of my first miscarriage came back to me clearly and I fell into a severe depression. I couldn't believe this was happening to me twice in such a short time-span, and, as a result, now I was left with an abnormal fear of pregnancy. I never was able to conceive again, due to what I believe was a psychological shut-down of my reproductive facilities, for I felt that I would never be able to carry to term. The ironic thing about it was that I simultaneously became obsessed with the notion of becoming pregnant.

14

FEELINGS OF ISOLATION

My parents accepted Edward and Pamela into the family almost from the beginning. Pamela was such a sweet child and neither they, nor my brothers and their families could resist her. Mom and Dad both adored Edward. He was different from anyone they were used to because he, Edward, possessed every quality of gentility and quietude that was inherently hidden or non-existent in a Roth or Steiner male. Edward never suffered from my father's abuse, and therefore responded very affectionately to Dad's infatuation with him. Similarly, Edward was completely charmed by my mother's youthful and energetic personality, as well as by their shared characteristic of self-restraint. She was very sophisticated, intelligent, and positive – all the things he never had a chance to see in his own mother – and he appreciated her immeasurably for these qualities. But it was a different story regarding my brothers.

Edward never had a brother and had spent his youth among the highly disciplined people of Switzerland. He had left his best friends behind, and although he had no close male-to-male friendships in Montreal he found little in common with my brothers. Steven and Marc didn't have any closely-bonded relationships with men either, so based on all of these factors, they didn't know how to establish any relationship with one another. Because he was the newcomer, Edward felt it was Steven and Marc's place to make the first social advances, based on his simple rules of common courtesy. Edward soon realized, however, that my brothers knew little about his unspoken code of manners.

One evening, when Edward and I were still living in Montreal with Pamela, we invited Steven and Sandra for supper. Unfortunately, the men got into a heated discussion on politics. Steven was used to leading a conversation due to his belief that he was more knowledgeable on almost all topics than most people were, and proceeded to talk at Edward instead of with him. Edward was informed on the subject they were debating, and he didn't appreciate the bulldozing manner which Steven tried to impress him with. The evening was a fiasco and it marked the beginning of a habitual silence between Steven and Edward that has lasted until the present. Over the years, the two of them had many more opportunities to be in one another's company, whereupon Edward learned to intensely dislike and lose even more respect for Steven.

Matters weren't as bad initially, or for some time afterwards, between Marc and Edward. Marc wasn't nearly as abrasive as Steven, and he wasn't obsessed with earning a fortune and owning every expensive object he could get his hands on either. He was also eight years younger than Edward, and therefore willing to converse with him in a more respectful manner. However, because Edward noticed that Marc treated me with a certain measure of scorn, he learned to dislike him as well. What eventually made Edward completely indifferent towards them both was the manner in which they treated my father which was with absolutely no respect whatsoever. Edward felt that no matter what my father had done to them in the past, as adults they had the choice to not see him and therefore not expose their atrocious, rude behavior.

My mother, as usual, organized all sorts of family get-togethers, which were supposed to be affectionate gatherings during festive and traditional occasions. After Edward had been integrated in our family for two or three months, my brothers no longer made special allowances for his presence; so Edward had opportunities to witness vicious arguments which he told me were incredulous, owing to the fact they were between persons who professed that they loved one another. The fact that he was probably right about this observation made me feel very uneasy, because I had to start accepting that my family wasn't at all the cohesive unit we pretended it was.

Edward's negative opinion of my brothers was continuously reinforced by their conduct while they were guests in our house. Steven would spend days in the living-room without ever trying to exchange one word with Edward. He, Sandra, and the boys would arrive with piles of food and gifts, and then Steven would retreat to the living-room or the den alone, leaving Sandra and his sons to act as the attending visitors.

Marc and Alice were easier to get along with, but were very messy guests, leaving their belongings all over the house. They would also spend a large amount of time visiting friends who lived very close by, which Edward and I thought was rude. However, we liked these friends of theirs very much, and when they were all at our house together, we enjoyed Marc and Alice's presence much more. I really liked being with Sandra and Alice, but could never manage to have them to myself for very long, not even to speak to, because Steven or Marc wouldn't leave us alone. The people who made these family get-togethers at all pleasant were the children, outside visitors, and my parents. When my brothers and their families finally left after one of these lengthy stays, they never expressed their appreciation for our hospitality in the proper manner, so after a few years we simply stopped inviting them for Christmas.

Just prior to our very first Christmas together, Steven moved to Toronto with Sandra and the boys after losing his three Burger King franchises in Montreal as a result of a court battle that had left him bankrupt. He decided he could no longer tolerate the French/English language problems in Quebec, or the corporate tax structure. It was a difficult period for him because no one in the family offered any moral support. He was a performer – the only way he obtained any self-esteem – and everyone was angry with him. I secretly felt sorry for him at this time, even though he was used to the lack of support that was characteristic of our family. Besides, he already had some new scheme he was working on in Toronto.

About a week after my second miscarriage, I was in Montreal shopping with my mother and Pamela, where I took a severe fall on an icy spot in the parking lot of a shopping center. Because I felt fine once I picked myself up, I returned to the country that evening with Pamela and thought nothing further about it. The following day, while I was driving Pamela home from her skiing lesson, my back was so sore that I barely made it from the car to the house. The next morning when I awoke, I was stiff but it was only after Pamela had gone to school and Edward had left for work that I collapsed from a stabbing pain in my lower back, and found myself on the floor of the living-room. I was petrified.

After spending twenty minutes on the floor trying to reach the telephone wire so that I could knock the phone off the couch, I managed to call up a friend. She came over immediately and saw that, at this point, I couldn't move at all. She phoned Edward's office but he wasn't there, so she called my mother and asked her to try to continue to contact Edward. As soon as he heard what happened he rushed home, but that was hours later. My friend propped me up against the couch with pillows, but then had to leave me to go and pick up our daughters at the entrance to our lake where the school bus dropped them off. At my request, she took Pamela home with her because I didn't want her to be frightened by seeing me in this condition. Pamela had been very traumatized by my despondent behavior after the miscarriage, only a short ten days before this, and I didn't want to upset her again. Edward arrived home and spent a grueling hour trying to help me into bed. The pain was excruciating, and we weren't sure if I had broken anything. He called our family doctor, who prescribed some super strong pain-killers which Edward promptly went out to buy, and later on that evening Dr. Small came to the house to examine me. His diagnosis was that I either had a group of torn muscles at the base of my spine, or that I had a severely herniated disc in the same place.

Unfortunately, I had the latter condition. The pain level of this ailment is considered to be about the optimum that a person can endure. For me it was catastrophic. I didn't want to go to a hospital and have surgery, which eventually became an option. In order to survive on a day-to-day basis, I had to take mega-doses of painkillers, and I spent the following three months living through the most harrowing physical experience of my life.

I was unable to move for the most part of two and a half weeks. I discovered that there was a doctor in the Laurentians who had become a chiropractor. I promptly arranged an appointment with him. Edward, who was spending every second day at home with me, somehow managed to carry me to the car. He laid me down on the back seat, which was propped up on all sides with pillows, and drove me to the chiropractor. I was half-crazed from the pain and the drugs; moreover, I was humiliated by my debility, for, since my fall, I had been unable to even go to the bathroom without Edward's help. He carried me in to see the doctor, who performed a series of manipulations on me, after which I was able to painstakingly walk out of his office with Edward's help.

The chiropractor explained the seriousness of my injury and said that, for the most part, I would have to be bedridden for at least three months. Because I was so exhilarated by the fact that I could move into an upright position, I didn't grasp the reality of what he was saying. I spent the next two months confined to my bed. During the first month, Edward and my friend Lissy took care of Pamela, the house, and all of my needs. After that, between seeing visitors, I spent most of my time alone in bed, reading, sleeping, and thinking.

The book that I chose during my recovery period was Victor Hugo's *Les Miserables*. It is the finest piece of literature I had on hand, and the finest I have ever read, but it is a very desolate tale about a man's selfless devotion for someone he loved. Unfortunately, everything about the story made me think about my family and how disappointed I was with them. They called a couple of times while I was bedridden, but that was all. My mother phoned often, but when I asked her to come and stay with me, she explained that she couldn't leave my father. I could hardly believe her insensitivity or the fact that my father could be selfish enough to ask her not to come. My parents' reluctance to give me the attention I needed deepened the sense of despair I was already experiencing. I felt as if they either didn't love me, or they really didn't know how to love anyone selflessly.

As a result of their neglect, I once again became centered on the memory of Mathew and how I believed he had been the only one among them who had loved me in a meaningful way. Pamela was barely seven years old and had been more of a comfort to me over my miscarriage and this accident than all of the family combined. She would often lie on the bed with me just to keep me company, sometimes pretending to read stories to me. And Edward was so compassionate, even though he was extremely frightened by my debilitated physical and psychological condition; I noticed that it was wearing him down.

After about three months in bed, I finally felt better physically. But, after having had so much time to think, I was extremely depressed. My depression was accompanied by a feeling of loathing for my family that I had not known before, which reflected onto my relationship with Edward and Pamela in both negative and positive ways. I distanced myself emotionally from them for fear that they would treat me the way my family had. At the same time I began to think of Edward and Pamela as my primary family – before my parents and my —brothers – and that was a positive perspective.

Unfortunately, for the two following years, Edward's ex-wife decided to try and destroy our marriage. What enabled me to emotionally survive that period was a weekend neighbour who had two adopted children and one biological child, who explained to me that she loved her adopted children as much as her natural child. I will be forever grateful for her sympathetic words because she had once also understood what it was like to feel as I did.

15

THE ROAD TO HEALING

During the two, trying years of court battles with Edward's ex-wife life otherwise went along quite smoothly for us. I established a little housecleaning business with a new friend, and Edward began to do extremely well at work. We continued to see my brothers and their families, but less frequently because they lived in Toronto and, besides the distance factor, everyone was too busy with their own lives to see one another anyway.

While Steven, Sandra, and the boys lived in Toronto, they became more intimate with Marc and Alice because of their close proximity. My parents drove to Toronto quite often to stay for the weekend, particularly after Marc and Alice had their first son, Adam. He was a new hope for the family, and for the first time Steven relished having a child in his life.

It didn't take Steven long to get back on the high road of achievement, and within two years he had built a multi-faceted and highly successful business empire in computer systems and insurance for car dealers. His habitual restlessness began to express itself as soon as he started to earn a lot of money, which was reflected in his moving three times in the four years he lived in Toronto. He was always upgrading his homes no matter what the emotional costs to his family. He also purchased a large number of extremely expensive cars and displayed them in prominent positions in front of these homes.

Marc, on the other hand, was as stable as Dad. He had no delusions of grandeur, was devoted to being an architect, and, after working for large companies for the first few years of his profession, landed a position as the permanent Project Architect for a large college in Toronto. Alice stayed home with Adam for six months then returned to her job. I noticed how much respect my brothers gave her simply for doing that. I wondered what their views were on my remaining at home to raise Pamela, and also what they thought about Sandra, considering that she stayed home with her own children. This bothered me because I believed they felt I was inadequate by not working in an outside job. I was relieved that my brothers lived a bit further away, because that way we wouldn't have to see one another as often and I would not have to feel guilty about it.

Two years after they moved to Toronto, Steven and Sandra prepared to host Ronnie's Bar Mitzvah. I remember that day vividly, as it was the only get-together that I could recall in recent years that was a family success. We were there to honour one of the children, and we were all so proud. Everyone in the family sat in the front row of the temple gazing lovingly at Ronnie, sensing his nervousness and silently giving our support.

I began to slip into a trance as I watched him up at the podium, and all of a sudden it all came back to me. I was in our community synagogue twenty-one years earlier, watching Mathew chant from the Torah. I became so overwhelmed with grief that, for a moment I thought I would faint, and it took all of my self-control not to leave the temple. Pamela was sitting beside me and asked me why I was crying, to which I responded that I was so elated that I couldn't help but cry. She believed me, but Edward knew how I really felt. For an instant I also thought I detected a far-off look in my mother's eyes, and I wondered if she was perhaps reliving that same moment with me. The entire ceremony was extremely difficult to witness, and I felt so guilty for not really being with Ronnie on this very special day.

As we stood around talking to people on the lawn prior to the reception, I drifted away from the crowd and watched my family from a distance. I felt totally isolated and had a flashback of Mathew's funeral. I was also suddenly struck by the disturbing revelation that I couldn't remember a single detail about Marc's Bar Mitzvah, which had taken place a little over a year after Mathew was killed. I had always prided myself on my exceptional memory, and it frightened me that no matter how hard I concentrated I still couldn't recall the events of that day. Years later, while undergoing therapy, I discovered that I had blanked out that day and, in actuality, wasn't consciously aware of what was happening during Marc's Bar Mitzvah ceremony.

It was during Ronnie's reception that I vowed to do something about my seemingly unresolved state of grief. I decided that I would write this book and that I would seek out professional help. I pursued both endeavors without my family's knowledge.

When Adam was four years old, Marc and Alice had their second son, Saul. Steven and Sandra moved to Florida. Steven bought out half of the parent company he represented then went on a spending spree with the money he made. He purchased a magnificent home, acquired several of the most expensive cars on the market, and built a one-hundred and twenty-foot yacht on which he entertained friends and family, while never once having the courtesy of inviting Edward, Pamela, and I. He even bought a Challenger jet to travel around the country, which nurtured his obsessive need for gaining everyone's esteem over his successes.

Marc and Alice, both of whom remained as stable as ever, worked at their respective professions and stayed in Toronto. They found a splendid old house before real estate prices skyrocketed and renovated it from top to bottom. They visited with Steven and Sandra frequently – Steven paid for everything – and they convinced themselves that they held a mutual respect for one another based on this convenient arrangement. In actuality, it was Marc and Alice's children that really enchanted Steven, providing the link between the two men. In fact, Adam proved to be an incredibly loving, prodigious, and sensitive child; Steven gravitated towards him, as did everyone, because of his saintly qualities.

During this three year period, Edward and I purchased a few chalets that we renovated with the help of contractors, and started up a rental business for ski and lake lovers. This business endeavor proved to be a big success for us and became, and has remained, my major occupation.

At the beginning of nineteen eighty-seven, I arranged a meeting with Professor Sommer, the Coordinator of the Creative Writing Program at Concordia University, to inquire about how one went about writing a book. He told me that if I was serious about the project – he emphasized the magnitude of such a goal – that I should begin by jotting down notes and collecting them, eventually start expanding on them, and, that if I persevered, with time they would take on the form of a book. He advised me not to pay too much attention to formal structure, but to concentrate instead on content and feelings, and not to force myself to write in chronological sequence. Before I left his office, Professor Sommer also gave me the name of a freelance editor whom he suggested I contact when the bulk of my manuscript was written. He was so inspiring that I began my book project the next day and discovered it to be the wisest thing I could have done. It was also the most challenging and rigorous project I have ever embarked upon on a long-term basis, but, nonetheless, the most productive medium with which I have exorcized most of my grief over Mathew.

Almost six months later, I found a therapist through the help of a friend, and began bi-monthly sessions. During the course of my therapy, I became aware that there was a great deal more mending to be done than I had thought there was, and I worked out many more issues with Keith, my therapist, besides Mathew's death.

I underwent an in-depth analysis of my entire family's background, and it was through this analysis, my personal effort, and my writing that I was able to begin to understand myself and my family. Keith helped me to realize that my mother had been totally unequipped emotionally to deal with the death of her brother Mathew. Her own mother had died from the shock of the news and there was no one there to comfort —her – at least that's what she concluded. She was never given the solace she so desperately needed from my grandmother, and therefore couldn't relieve any of her own grief through the help of others, so her anguish remained pent-up inside of her.

Then when she lost her son, the only way that she felt she could survive was to remain silent because she had no idea how to discuss her loss with anyone. By doing this, my mother, unconsciously, abandoned us. My father was never given a chance to help her in any effective way, and all the traumas that my brothers and I individually suffered after Mathew's death and later on in life were undealt with – always strewn aside as being incidental compared to my mother's grief over the loss of her son.

How did we react to this situation? Steven absorbed our father's rage and aggression, and alienated himself from everyone by his arrogant and cruel manner, which I began to understand, was one of his ways of covering up his anguish. Marc also absorbed our father's rage, but luckily he was also influenced by my mother's sensitive, maternal qualities, which were reflected later on in his behavior towards his own children. Although I too was influenced by my mother's loving manner, I left home tormented and angry, and with a tremendous fear of intimacy due to my anxiety over the possibility of loss.

With Keith's help, I became aware that I felt as if the individual members of my family no longer truly loved me from the time that I was about twenty years old. Steven was never really civil to me again from age twenty on, and over the years Marc became more aggressive. I was certain that Marc harboured anger and resentment towards me for preferring Mathew over him when we were children; and, as he and I had never discussed this subject together as we grew older, these pent-up feelings intensified.

Strangely enough, we all married someone who was similar in character to my mother. Sandra was a totally supportive and affectionate woman who feigned emotional reserve, and who willingly endured all kinds of subtle abuse from Steven because she was prepared to be his emotional vehicle. I also became aware that Alice was similar to Sandra in her personal attributes as well, possessing a sincere quality of self-restraint, although their marriage was more egalitarian. Edward also was a person of grace and reserve, but as a result of our marriage – by being subjected to my family for so many years – he has discovered many of his own family problems by helping me work through mine.

My father, on the other hand, has never stopped paying for the way he treated my brothers and I as children. Although, to a large degree, I have forgiven him, but my brothers never have. When Mathew died, he lost a part of my mother's devotion that he never got back, but he also lost my brothers' respect and affection; and, as the years progressed, they continuously displayed disregard for his feelings and scorn for his views. Perhaps he was also afraid of losing my affection, so, to protect himself, he treated me aggressively during my —youth – his method of defense against any further rejection. Unknown to him, as I grew older, I often felt sympathetic towards my father, as we often both felt unloved by most of the family members.

I believe Dad subconsciously took it upon himself to do a great deal of emotional work for my mother. Five years after Mathew was killed, and just before I got married, he fell into his first of many depressions. After his father and mother died, he suffered from severe depressions which lasted for months. When he was fifty-one, he had his gall-bladder removed. Then, when he was in his sixties, he suffered three heart attacks, had a triple by-pass operation, and had major surgery to connect a large artery from his torso to his leg in order not to lose a foot. This last operation was partly a reaction to Steven's losing his fortune. I now believe that Dad's depressions were his way of avoiding the reality of his life's traumas. I also believe that his depressions and illnesses were his way of empathetically suffering for my mother, as well as a method of confirming her love and devotion because she had to take care of him through all of these ailments.

It became clear to me that their behaviour was a game my parents unconsciously played. When I was ill or depressed, my mother would insist that either my father wouldn't allow her to come and stay overnight, or that he didn't want her to leave him all alone. In other words he acted as her scapegoat. Sometimes, she would insist that she couldn't possibly leave my father on his own, and thereby reinforced his need for her.

Over the years, there were many important experiences my family could have shared that would have made a great difference in our entire relationship. But, most important of all, I could have shared the experience of losing a brother with my mother. She could never have imagined how many times I looked her in the face knowing that she understood my anguish, while at the same time realizing that she wouldn't help me. She knew exactly how I felt, but was simply incapable of doing anything about it; and it is only recently that I have forgiven her for that. By ridding myself of most of my grief over Mathew through analysis and through my writing, I have been able to feel a deep and sincere compassion for her – a compassion which I now even extend to strangers.

My mother had too many demands made on her when my brothers and I were younger, and so she loved us all as best she could. Perhaps because she didn't easily accept our shortcomings, I, in turn, didn't readily accept anyone else's incapacities until very recently. Through extensive reading, I've come to the conclusion that Mathew was probably my soul mate or my guardian angel. Because he infused me with so much love, no one understood – not even me – that he had become much more than a brother to me, for he nourished my spirit in an almost supernatural way. When he was taken from me, the only other person whose love I thought I could depend on became unavailable to me. I have spent all of these years working out the feeling of being incompletely loved and abandoned.

16

CENTER FOR SIBLING LOSS

I have a cousin, Alex, with whom I have always been especially close, who has a gentle and sensitive nature. I needed to tell someone in the family about the book I was writing, so, after I had been actively compiling my notes for a couple of years, I decided to confide in him. A year later, he mailed me an article that appeared in People magazine in March of 1987 concerning a center which two psychologists had opened in Chicago, called the Rothman-Cole Center for Sibling Loss. The article detailed a variety of interesting points on the topic of sibling loss, which convinced me that writing my memoir was the correct thing to do. It also confirmed that many of my unvoiced suspicions were true regarding people like me who had lost a sibling.

Doctor Rothman and his colleague, Mr. Cole, had both lost siblings as children. The article commenced with a statement by Dr. Rothman who said that it had taken him twenty-five years to come to terms with the loss of his brother, and which assured me that I wasn't alone or crazy. He proceeded to profile the debilitating emotional price that children with unresolved grief had to pay, and added that these reactions affected their entire lives if not dealt with. He confirmed that these children suffer a double loss because they lose their parents as well, either for a brief or indefinite period of time. Dr. Rothman also mentioned that it was common for surviving siblings to end up unmarried, and that if they did marry they were less likely to have children, which immediately explained to me my own difficulties in having a child. This last point was an additional factor a sister had to deal with, as opposed to a surviving brother, as brothers, of course, didn't have to bear children. The reason for these siblings to end their lives unmarried, or without children, Dr. Rothman said, was that they were terrified of running the risk of further loss in their lives. It had been proven that the chance of surviving siblings growing up without problems of an extreme nature were rare; and because siblings greatly shape each other's personalities, the surviving siblings' intellectual, emotional, and social growth would probably be stunted. He stressed that children less than ten years of age and adolescents were the most traumatized in instances of sibling loss.

Dr. Rothman went on to explain that he founded the center because of the "epidemic rise in child and adolescent deaths due to drugs, murder, and suicide." He added that there were no services anywhere that catered to surviving siblings, and that it was a desperately needed service. I recall clutching the magazine in relief and weeping out loud because this article was like a gift from God. I was not alone, or "abnormal and the revelations in this article are what motivated me to finish this book. Because Dr. Rothman and Mr. Cole both lost siblings, I decided that I could benefit by attending one of their weekend workshops, which were designed specifically for people who needed their specialized grief-therapy services.

At the same time that I received the article in People magazine, I was deeply involved with my therapist trying to work out my depressed state over many issues, of which the primary ones were the effects Mathew's death had on me and my family's refusal to openly confront our grief. Keith's group of colleagues held what was considered to be highly unconventional, but, nevertheless, very successful "spiritual healing" weekends. He suggested that the time was ideal for me to attend one. I told him about my desire to enroll in the Rothman-Cole Center workshop and that if I did I couldn't afford to take the spiritual workshop as well. Keith informed me that it was fortunate that these events were happening within six weeks of one another, and that I would greatly benefit the most if I could attend both in that short time span. He convinced me to partake in both workshops, then arranged for me to pay for the spiritual weekend in installments. Similarly, the Rothman-Cole Center accepted a slightly lower fee due to the fact that I had to fly to Chicago, and because I explained to them that I was also enrolling in the other workshop.

I won't detail the spiritual weekend as it would take too much explanation. In essence, we were a group of thirty people who did yoga exercises, chanting, and meditations together. However, I will say that the workshop left me with some sense of resolution and self-confidence. Keith had shown me that, despite my guise as a self-assured woman, I was in fact an extremely sensitive and fragile person who needed a great deal of tenderness to overcome all the years in which I had not received any.

Six weeks later, in the spring of 1988, I flew to Chicago to spend thirty hours of intensive work on resolving my pent up grief over the loss of my brother Mathew. The workshop was one of the most constructive and significant experiences of my life, and afterwards I felt like a different person. It was also the most difficult and excruciatingly painful few days I have ever spent voluntarily.

At the Rothman-Cole Center, I was faced with a group of seven women who had also lost siblings – two of them lost more than one – through various circumstances. The women's ages ranged from twenty-three to fifty. The twenty-three year old had lost a brother who committed suicide only five years earlier, while the fifty-year-old had lost two siblings who died of meningitis, forty and forty-three years earlier, respectively. The rest of us had lost siblings by way of accidents.

The workshop was conducted by three therapists including Dr. Rothman, his wife, and another male psychologist. Throughout the entire weekend the most unique collection of meditative music was played continuously, full of subliminal messages pertinent to the work we were involved in. Our activities included art therapy, which we then critiqued in writing; yogic exercise; massage sessions; group singing; and, most difficult of all, meditation sessions and verbal critiques of our own and one another's artwork.

For the first time, I had the opportunity to witness adults release their emotions in a way that I had never allowed myself to do, especially not in the company of others. A few of the women completely broke down and began screaming and sobbing uncontrollably, and, guided by the therapists, I had the chance to be able to comfort and physically hold these women in their worst moments.

While I was at the Rothman-Cole Center, I discovered four very important things about myself. To begin with, I realized that I didn't have to feel remorse about being relieved of my own grief while in the company of others who were as tormented as I was. Secondly, I became aware that, since Mathew's death, whenever a woman tried to comfort me by holding me in her arms, I backed away emotionally and prevented it from happening. Thirdly, it became clear to me that in my mind Mathew had been more than just a brother to me. Because he had unconditionally accepted and loved me, much of the nurturing attention that I didn't assimilate from my mother and my father I received from him.

Finally, one of the therapists explained to me what my "out of body" experiences were all about. During a very intense and painful meditation, Dr. Rothman's colleague approached me and lightly touched my hand, which instantly pulled me out of a trance. He said, "Laura, get back in your body because I can see you leaving," assuring me at the same time that he would speak about this incident later.

Towards the end of the meditation there was a rest period which was followed by a short break. During the rest period, the psychologist asked me if I had ever undergone any "out of body" experiences before this. I recounted those incidents after Mathew died when, at night, I would find myself seated in my chair, looking in horror at my body which was lying in bed across the room. I also told him that over the last twenty years I often felt as if I simply wasn't "inside myself." He began by citing the example of how a large portion of the population functioned out of their bodies quite frequently. One simply had to walk downtown anywhere in a large city and watch the people rushing about to observe that many of them simply "weren't there." I noticed this for years, always referring to this phenomenon as being "in your head" as opposed to being consciously aware of your surroundings. The psychologist also explained that documentation had shown that people were fully capable of transcending their bodies, but that if a person was "out of body" under certain conditions for too long they could, in fact, die. He said that I used this method as a safety valve to avoid the pain of Mathew's death, but added that, unfortunately, it was a dangerous technique which didn't resolve anything because I wasn't being guided through it. I also admitted that during the meditation I was in such intense emotional anguish that I probably was trying to "leave" subconsciously. He said that he noticed that, at the time, I practically stopped breathing, turned completely white, and been stone cold when he touched me; then he advised me not to try to invoke this method again, if at all possible.

After my talk with the psychologist, I made a commitment to myself to stop using this escape method and to remain grounded in my body, so that I could consciously deal with my problems – after all, I did have Keith in Montreal, as well as a very supportive husband. Oddly enough, when I next saw Keith – before I had the chance to speak of my experiences in Chicago – he greeted me by saying, "Welcome back Laura. I sense that you are completely present for the first time." I was astounded by his almost supernatural perception, and our work together was even more successful from then on.

I left Chicago having made one important friend out of the group of seven women, as well as with the comfort of realizing that I was not alone in my grief. I knew that thousands of people everywhere had lost siblings, but until that weekend I had never come into contact with anyone who knew what my brothers and I had been through, although I have met many such people since then.

There were multiple benefits to having gone to that weekend workshop. One breakthrough was that I became capable of comforting other people who were suffering through a death in their family. Before the Rothman-Cole workshop, I was unable to attend funerals without becoming totally centered on my own grief. A year after I returned from Chicago, I found myself in the home of friends of a friend who recently lost their twelve year old son, Jimmy, a month earlier. Jimmy's one remaining kidney had failed and he died in his parents' arms. Their five year old daughter, Sonia, was exhibiting extremely bizarre after-effects which they didn't know how to handle, so I went to see the parents after our mutual friend had approached me and asked me if I could offer any help. Jane, his five year old, was Sonia's best friend, and was becoming affected by Sonia's reaction to her grief over the loss of her brother. I drove to their home and informed the parents about the Rothman-Cole Center – amazed that I could even talk to them about losing their child.

Sonia's father worked for an airline and arranged for his daughter to be flown to Chicago every week, but Dr. Rothman advised him that the trips would be too exhausting for such a young child and that he and his wife should search for help closer to home. On my suggestion, they decided to work with Keith. Fortunately, they were comfortable with him, and their sessions in family grief-therapy were most successful.

Another significant benefit of my visit to the Rothman-Cole Center was that I noticed a dramatic change in my character. For the first time, I was able to comfort my mother during the rare occasions that she mentioned Mathew to me, after which she would immediately fall to pieces. By just speaking some tender words to her, or by touching or holding her, she would suddenly feel better which made me feel incredibly uplifted. I realized that I was finally capable of exhibiting compassion that either wasn't there before, or that I hadn't been able to express. And the most crucial test of my newfound inner strength was my ability to endure finding my dear friend and neighbour, David, dead in his car, and not lose my mind over it. I even composed and recited the eulogy at his funeral in front of a few hundred people without falling apart.

17

TRANSITION

About six months after attending the Rothman-Cole Center, I had a serious falling out with Marc. I asked him if it disturbed him that he, Alice, and the boys had frequent opportunity to spend time with my parents and Steven's family during the winter months, while never spending any with Edward, Pamela, and I. When he answered that, quite frankly, he didn't give a damn, even I was astounded at my reaction. I felt completely rejected and became hysterical once I hung up the phone. Edward didn't know how to calm me down, except that when Alice called back to apologize, Edward told her that I had no desire to speak to either one of them and that, as far as he was concerned, my brothers were bastards who didn't deserve the time of day from me.

Marc followed up this incident with a letter that was so loathsome that even Keith was shocked at the amount of pain and rage it expressed – especially because so much of it was directed at me. I, in turn, wrote a long reply to Marc, made copies of both letters, and then sent one of each to my parents, Steven, and Sandra, as I referred to them all in one way or another. My mother called me, and I screamed at her explaining that I was almost at the end of my rope with our family, that I was sick and tired of her inability to try and encourage a closeness between her children, and that I was seriously deliberating whether or not I ever wanted to see any of them again. Intending to be helpful, Steven called me, but of course he didn't have any idea of how to handle this. After thirty seconds on the phone, he started criticizing and demeaning me, and the only reason I listened to his tirade of insults was his mention of how I messed up so many aspects of my life when I was in my teens and my early twenties. For the first time, I realized that Steven's present perception of me was of who I was twenty-five years ago. Although I had always suspected this, I had thought it was too ridiculous to be possible.

That winter, when Mom approached Marc about our fight, his response was that I preferred Mathew to him when we were kids, and that he wasn't going to make any effort to reconcile our differences. The impact of my reaction to my argument with Marc captured the attention of Sandra and Alice, who both came to see me a month after receiving copies of their respective letters. Alice brought Saul with her from Toronto, so my mother accompanied all of them so that she could take care of him while we girls talked. I laughed sadly to myself as my sisters-in-law arrived, realizing they were at my home representing my brothers, which made me feel even more isolated than usual.

Sandra, Alice, and I walked around the lake, my two sisters-in-law keeping close to one another at all times. On our way back, as we approached the house, I suggested that we go instead to a neighbour's grounds and continue with what was becoming a very serious and important conversation. After all, it was the first time that the three of us had ever been alone together, as well as the first time that either of them had demonstrated any real concern towards me. By talking about my brothers and me as children, I released a great deal of my pent-up grief on this occasion, even though I was standing about ten feet away from my two sisters-in-law who were clutching on to each other and weeping while they listened to me. They didn't even come over to try and hold —me – I had to approach them! I began to realize that because they had been living with my brothers for such a long time, they were probably used to dealing with their own grief without help from their husbands. At one point in the conversation, they both mentioned that "everyone has to suffer through their own sorrows alone," to which I responded that I felt terribly sorry for them if that was what they really believed. In fact, more often than not over the years they had become empaths for my brothers' emotional stresses, especially Sandra for Steven.

After my sisters-in-law left, I spent many days thinking about these two women. At the beginning of her affair with Marc, Alice confided to me that she never had a close relationship with her mother. She had been in awe of her father and had an estranged relationship with her brother and his wife. Sandra told me that she had been raised mainly by her grandmother, who looked after her while her mother went out to work, and that she didn't have a father in her life until she was ten or eleven years old. Sandra's mother had given birth to her following an affair that broke up shortly afterwards, and so she never knew her biological father. Her step-father, Mr. MacNamara, was looked upon as Sandra's real father – the one we all knew and loved – but no one in our family had ever spoken of how she had been affected by her early years. Both of these women lost their fathers within seven years prior to our meeting at the lake, and only Alice's mother was still alive. Sandra's mother died a year and a half after her father had.

This all explained the intense connection they had with my brothers, but, more importantly, how inexperienced they were in dealing with women. And, as it turned out, they each bore sons and no daughters. After that meeting at my house in the country, we never had the chance to be alone together again or to speak to one another privately.

Steven's business failed that year, but this time Sandra couldn't cope with the upheaval. This was the third one she experienced while being married to my brother. She flew to Ontario, where Kevin and Ronnie were living, first, to help Kevin get settled into a new apartment, and second, to be close to Ronnie in his private school in northern Ontario. She also went so she could see her psychiatrist. Dr. Corry was the only physician she trusted to help her out of her suicidal state of mind. He admitted her to a psychiatric facility for two months where she received excellent care. Steven remained in Florida throughout her ordeal, mainly because of his continuously required presence during legal proceedings regarding his bankruptcy. Sandra confessed to me that she wasn't sure if she could ever go back to my brother. However, she eventually did return to him because, through therapy, she realized that she encouraged Steven's manic behavior over the years by accepting his totally erratic, demanding, and emotionally destructive manner towards everyone. However, this time she was committed to finding a job without his help and reconstructing a positive self-image.

I was completely distraught by Sandra's psychological breakdown, and took it upon myself to be as supportive as she would allow me to. Over a period of about sixty days, I called her every second day to listen to her talk about her life. I then gave her feedback, and, at times, even cried along with her. We learned more about one another in those two months than we had in the previous eighteen years. During this period, I found out how much I loved her and how much I sympathized with her based on my sincere concern for her well-being, which I often communicated to her. As a result, we now have a mutual sympathetic understanding that wasn't apparent before.

I found myself constantly worrying about everyone in Steven's and Sandra's immediate family circle. Kevin had no self-confidence because he had only worked for Steven's companies. Ronnie was fortunate to be away at school both prior to and then during Steven's business upheaval – a very intelligent ploy on Sandra's part to remove him physically from his father's influence – and he was the only person in the family who loved everyone and was deeply loved by them in return; in that way, he reminded me so much of Mathew. But he had to cope with the fact that his friends knew about Steven's business failure. It was a scandalous affair that almost landed my brother in jail, and the story was plastered all over the newspapers. Steven treated many people poorly over the years, and his enemies were now out to get him and were doing anything they could to make his life miserable. Because Steven was all alone in Florida without much personal support from anyone, I innately knew that Ronnie was traumatized over his Dad's problems.

I sent a letter to Ronnie asking him to write his father, and to give Steven his assurance that he loved him, no matter what he had done. I knew that Ronnie in actuality felt that way, but that he might not make the effort to do it. Kevin was enraged at Steven and would definitely not communicate with him unless absolutely necessary and Sandra was trying to sort out her own problems. My mother kept in close contact with Steven throughout this entire ordeal, but my father was unable to lend much sympathy. He was in a state of shock over Steven's business failure and was too angry to call and offer him a reassuring word. Marc, who had professed his devotion for Steven in that awful letter he sent me nine months earlier, never went to Florida to console Steven; although, he did call to ask Steven if he wanted him to fly down. When Steven replied that this was unnecessary, Marc didn't have the sensitivity to see past his brother's words and simply go down to stay with him for a while.

I was fascinated by this sudden concern I had for Steven, although it all became clear eventually as to why I felt this way. Despite how much I tried not to admit it to myself, I still loved him. And, although I knew I would never again risk being abused by him, I still wanted some sort of connection with him, so I was trying to relay some of that love via other people. Ironically, when I fantasized about trying to re-capture some of the affection we once had, I usually visualized myself attacking him bodily and beating him into the ground, which made me aware of the anger I still harboured against him. I hoped that one day that hostility would leave me and that Steven would forgive me for loving Mathew more than I loved him – and for whatever else he imagined I had done to him. Similarly, I hoped that someday I would forgive him for all the abuse he directed at me and that I would not be affected by it anymore.

In the spring of 1989, my parents' fiftieth wedding anniversary – an event to be held in June – was fast approaching. If Steven had been financially secure, it would not have surprised me to hear he rented the "Love Boat" for the celebration and invited hundreds of people. For once, the thought of such pomp didn't gall me the way it usually did, because he would have made these arrangements primarily out of love and not for show, but of course this was not going to happen.

Because Marc was not used to being the host on family occasions – that task had always fallen on either Steven or I – it was up to me to organize the event. After convincing Edward to receive my brothers in our house, I decided to hold a surprise party for my parents. It took several weeks of planning and sneaking around to arrange the party. My mother mentioned to me that her only anniversary wish was to have her children and their families together, so I told her that I would do that for her. I invited twenty people who had attended my parents' wedding fifty years earlier. Many other people, mainly friends of theirs whom I wanted to invite, had already passed away. Fifteen of the guests showed up, and some of them even flew in from out of town. I called a caterer and Edward bought a tape with all the beautiful old songs that Mom and Dad adored, including the Anniversary Waltz. We borrowed our neighbour's stereo system as the sound was better than ours, and decided to play my parents' favourite song as they walked in the door.

The house and grounds were lavishly decorated, and Mom and Dad's fifteen friends all arrived at our doorstep without my parents' knowledge. Marc, who arrived long before Mom and Dad, was as warm and loving as he could be towards me, even though we never made up after our argument in the autumn. Steven and Sandra drove my parents to the party. We managed to conceal all the other cars by parking them at various neighbour's houses, and the guests all hid in our bedroom. As Mom and Dad walked through the door, Edward turned on the music while everyone filed out simultaneously singing "Happy Anniversary" and throwing confetti at my parents. It was one of those rare, precious moments that I'll remember with joy for the rest of my life. Everything went perfectly.

During the afternoon, I dedicated the song "The Rose" to my parents. My brothers and I and our spouses all took turns dancing with one another with my parents waltzing together at the end. While I was dancing with Marc, he held me tightly and whispered in my ear that he loved me. I felt for an instant that I would pass out, for he had never said this to me before. I whispered back that I loved him too, and although we still have many differences, our relationship changed greatly for the better from that moment on. What was also marvelous about the party was that there was peace and harmony between us all, for my parents' sake. The anniversary photographs prove that, for the first time in twenty-five years, my mother displayed her radiant smile – the one I remembered before Mathew was killed, the one I had never seen since then. Seeing her smile made the entire affair worthwhile, because, for a few hours, my mother forgot her unspoken vow to never allow herself to be as happy as she was before Mathew's death. It was an absolutely splendid day, apparently as fine, as sunny, and as beautiful as the one they were married on. When all the guests had left, Mom and Dad said that in all their years together they never experienced a celebration in which they had derived such pleasure.

18

FAMILIES AND SIBLINGS

When we, as siblings, are children living together at home, we constantly learn about one another, our parents, and how we all interrelate through the processes of observation and communication. We live in the same house, often go to the same —school – thereby partake in some knowledge of each other outside of the family —home – and we share the same parents. Every member of the family unit is conscious of all the different rules of conduct each has to follow. As children, we usually eat and sleep at similar hours and are almost always aware of what the other family members are doing. This structure gives the individuals in the family group intimate information about one another. We are forced together, so to speak, and for peace to prevail there has to be a constant effort to continue a harmonious, or at least reasonable, coexistence.

As we grow up and eventually move out on our own, if our parents don't realize that a determined effort must be made by all the family members to continue in this common awareness of one another, we slowly but surely drift apart. We develop our own personal environments, ones that are often very different from the mutual one we once shared. Other people become integral parts of our lives – friends, husbands and wives, and their respective families – people who don't have first-hand knowledge of the original core group, or how it functioned. And as a result, we flow into different activities and interests that our own family never engaged in. Although all of these changes and developments are normal and necessary, if the original family members don't remain in close touch during this transition, the family's cohesive nature will rapidly deteriorate. If we siblings don't continue to relate our feelings and growth experiences to one another, we tend to misinterpret our individual emotional reactions based on how we interrelated in our youth, even though each person's reactions have probably changed dramatically over the years. The way we have become is not necessarily the way we were. Our mutual responses are, more often than not, completely inaccurate and our misinterpretations become exaggerated over time. We proceed to express our resulting anger cruelly upon one another, or we retreat to our respective environments and vent our repressed anger at an inappropriate time later on; or, even worse, on to the wrong people altogether – people who aren't even involved. The old advantage of being "forced together," and thereby having to resolve many of our differences, is no longer there.

Communication is the only tool we have at our disposal that gives us the chance to feel safe again, and to learn, and to understand one another again. But this is the tool most people have the greatest difficulty with. To communicate is to risk exposing oneself to others – to undress one's emotions. But we don't trust people because we are afraid that if we reveal our true selves, the listeners will be able to betray us with the knowledge we give them; therefore, more often than not, we choose not to do this. As time goes by and our misinterpretations are blown out of proportion, our anger and cool reserve become highly developed methods of self-defense. Moreover, after a period of many years, these negative feelings become so integrated into our thought patterns that we often become distant and embittered towards one another.

In the case of my own family, as is true of many families, there was never a great deal of communication despite the excessive amount of screaming and verbal exchange that occurred. At the precise time when our parents would probably have been aware of the effort needed to keep my brothers and I in close contact, Mathew was killed. Steven and I were already drifting apart, while Marc, unfortunately, was at the age when he was still very close to Mathew. Just trying to keep us all sane through this tragedy was almost impossible for my parents, let alone any endeavor on their part to maintain communication between my brothers and me. No one realized how estranged everyone in the family was becoming. Because we were all so terrified of suffering any more pain than we were already experiencing, we didn't understand that talking would be less painful than silence.

Many people can coast comfortably in this deluded state, and one can even spend one's whole life this way. For those among us who don't coast well, this mode of existence is costly for it leaves its participants feeling terribly lonely and spiritually deprived. In my own case, I discovered once I became a mature adult that I had taken my childhood experiences with my family very seriously. In my mind, I completely integrated the concept of "family" as a sacred and indestructible entity that could overcome anything – an entity that would always be there as the need arose for any of its individual members. After all, I had originated within this family unit and they were the most important people during the first twenty years of my life. Although I'm grateful that adulthood has brought me wisdom, I have never accepted its ultimate disillusionment: the unexpected abandonment of my family's emotional support due to our inability to deal with the death of one of our family members.

I have always believed that if I could have been able to share my life experiences with them, including my deepest despair, I would have been able to resolve much of my grief and therefore found great solace. I'm aware that nobody ever knows anyone very well, but I believed that my family members had a special advantage over all other people because they were the only ones who knew me from the very beginning.

We carried on what became the family tradition of not communicating. We never shared a single word about the greatest mutual tragedy of our lives. Although we have often been together physically, we always seem to be watching each other from a distance on these occasions. The love we still hold for one another has always been there hidden deep inside us, no matter how illusive, but our fears always got the better of us. Dr. Jampolski expresses perfectly in the title of one of his books what I have always wished my family would have understood: *Love is Letting Go of Fear*.

I've noticed recently that we are all mellowing, and I also realize that some of us are trying to be considerate to one another. Ever since my parents' fiftieth wedding anniversary, Marc has made a noticeable effort to reconcile, and occasionally he and Edward converse in a pleasant manner. Perhaps in the near future, I won't have to keep wishing that Steven and I can be in one another's company and feel comfortable about it.

In the past, my brothers and I have expressed our love for each other through each other's children: Marc towards Pamela; I at first towards Kevin and Ronnie, and then eventually towards Adam and Saul; and Steven towards Marc's two boys, as he was unable to be really affectionate with his own children when they were small. Unfortunately, our past negative behavior is already etched into our kids memories – hopefully not permanently – particularly Kevin, Ronnie, and Pamela who are now twenty-six, nineteen, and fifteen years old, respectively. I have lived in a small country community for over ten years now and regret having to look with envy at the strong, affectionate, family ties around me. They personify what I had hoped for my own family, but I'm finally accepting that we may never be quite like them.

However, I am learning to tolerate the characteristics about my family that have always greatly upset me. These include trying to accept my father's awe of wealth, his continual discontentment, and his unending self-centeredness. I've also had to overlook my mother's inability to encourage peace between her children, as well as her incapacity to have a meaningful emotional exchange with me or to give me any real comfort. In addition to this, I'm slowly learning to endure my brothers' hostility by recognizing that their anger is an expression of their own unresolved pain, and will continue trying to feel compassion towards them because of it. Moreover, I've started to forgive my parents and my brothers for excluding Edward, Pamela, and I from family get-togethers. They felt we wouldn't enjoy one another's company, and therefore appeared to be insensitive and non-caring about how hurtful this might have been to the three of us.

The other things I'm still trying to work out are of a personal nature. I feel that if I had been more encouraged and helped more emotionally, I could have accomplished great things, but then I no longer have my old and often shallow opinions of "greatness." It was Edward who helped me clarify my views. I remember a heartwarming incident that happened one afternoon. He was lying on our bed reading while I was standing next to him putting on my make-up. I complained that I was feeling rather deficient about not generating any income into our household and letting such a heavy financial burden fall solely on his shoulders. He put down his book, and, without really looking up, said, "Don't be silly Laura, you've made an excellent effort with your little businesses. You have also done a splendid job buying our rental properties, which you have very cleverly and successfully transformed into more valuable buildings. All of your ventures have provided us with fantastic tax shelters. You are the dearest, brightest, most interesting and gifted person I've ever met. Unlike most people, who only know how to do a few things well, I'm amazed at how many talents you do have and how different they all are. And among those abilities, so much of what you do brings happiness to —others – that alone is a great gift. You're not the easiest person to live with, but I'm grateful to be the one who can make it possible for you to continue in all your endeavors. Just be secure in the fact that I love you and will always believe in you." I was overwhelmed by this commentary from my so-called "reticent husband." It was worth waiting all my life to hear someone say such marvelous things to me. I must add that this book would never have been completed without Edward's unfaltering support.

I will probably spend many more years coming to terms with the fact that I have never had a biological child, which, besides Mathew's death, has been the worst thing I've had to live with. Recently, I have discovered that dealing with infertility and the loss of pregnancies follows precisely the same recovery lines as losing a loved one – just knowing this is helping me cope with my situation. I will say, however, that raising Pamela has been an incredibly fulfilling experience for me. I have shared extraordinarily sensitive and meaningful moments with —her – moments when I believe that if she hadn't been in my life, I would have fallen apart. One of those memorable occasions happened quite recently. She was sitting at the dining-room table, asking me very discreetly if her father and I were still trying to have a baby. I told her that my chances were lessening because of my age. Looking right at me, she said, "You know Mom, I've somehow always believed that you and I were meant to be together, alone." God bless her! Perhaps my inability to have my own baby has been the Lord's way of teaching me that one can love any child as much as one's own.

CONCLUSION 1996

Having had Mathew in my life, the fact that he died, and my family's inability to deal with his death has affected every stage of my development. His enlightening presence in my childhood made me unaware of the emotional voids that existed in our home, and how those voids created greater and greater dissention between me and my other brothers. The shock of his death ruined my youth. Eventually, because I was never able to resolve it with anyone, I felt isolated from most people, but especially from Steven and Marc. Because I was blinded by grief, I didn't understand that our silence would result in a growing hostility and fear of one other.

My obsession with Mathew tainted every affair I ever had, for I compared the quality of my men's level of devotion to the quality of love I had received from Mathew despite the vast difference in both types of relationships, and it took me many years to realize how abnormal this was. As I grew into womanhood and began thinking about having a child, my thoughts continually focused on the possibility of reincarnating Mathew. I suspect that my inability to have my own child was due to a tremendous dread I subconsciously harboured that I would somehow lose that child because I had lost Mathew.

I know that it is easy to dramatize the past and to idolize the dead. However, after reassessing our lives over these past twenty-seven years, I can't help but imagine how vastly different our relationships and our paths would have been if Mathew had lived. Perhaps if I had always remained close to him – and indeed I'm sure I would have – I would never have had to endure so much suffering due to my personal traumas or my problems with my brothers, many of which I feel would simply not have developed if Mathew was still alive. My three brothers would have been intimate – I know it. And because Mathew was one of three male siblings, I believe he would have been able to affect his loving influence on all of us, and we probably would have been bonded in the way I always dreamed we would be. Of course this is all wishful thinking. I have now finally admitted to myself that many things didn't work out in this family the way I hoped they would, and as a result I was always disillusioned. My parents have been pretending for many years that our family relationships are satisfactory, while my brothers and I have just drifted farther and farther apart. The wall of silence between us has now become so established that I often feel little hope of breaking it down. I accept a large part of the blame for this situation, because I too have been guilty of participating. This memoir is my effort at ending my own silence.

In *The Power of Myth*, Joseph Campbell says, "Follow your bliss and don't be afraid, and doors will open where you didn't know where they were going to be." Composing my own book has proven to me that he is right. Many helpful people and useful information on dealing with death has literally fallen into my lap since I began this work. I have exorcized a great deal of my pain by undertaking this project, and although I've had to relive my past over and over again with every rewrite, I have gained insights I never had before. It has also amazed me to discover that the translation of my thoughts on to paper, when read, far exceeds having them float around in my mind. I would never have known this if I had not written this book.

Even though my family has not read this manuscript yet, I realized while writing that I felt as if I had been communicating with them, and that has given me a tremendous release. While preparing these last few pages, two lines of verse came to me; "For all the darkness that I've seen, I feel closer to you than I've ever been." I feel that they need no explanation.

CONCLUSION 2014 (CELEBRATION)

We've all come to realize that without the presence of problems, despair, and even evil, we would not recognize the great gifts of joy, peace, beauty and goodness around us. But we need a lot of help to get on the road to being well.

We have all come a long way in the last 50 years as regards helping one another and communicating with one another. For example, in the 60's and 70's homosexuals were hiding their orientation due to being victimized by the public. Some were even killed, simply because their sexual orientation was different. Post partum depression was scoffed at as the spoiled, childish attitude of a woman who didn't want to take care of her newborn. Help was so illusive in the 60's that recovery from most major traumas was almost impossible.

I am grateful for the universal compassion of people today, and with all the avenues of interaction available for those in need; the internet being paramount, and the ability to express, study, exchange and learn about the development and treatment of very serious issues. These avenues offer a huge support system to the suffering.

However, I've also learned that without a huge and continued effort to heal from life's upheavals, many things can never change. Recovering from enormous trauma, as in the sudden accidental death of my brother, became a kind of 'life endeavor' of mine which continues until to-day – not an obsession, but an endeavor. I am much better now, but still have that underlying sadness ... it will always be there, and I am always working on it.

Thank goodness I have a rich life filled with the love of my spouse, his family and grandchildren; culture and interesting, meaningful pastimes. I have extraordinary work endeavors, including being the creator and manager of a symphony orchestra (www.musiciansoftheworld.ca). I've been blessed with communication skills and the ability to write so that I could share my story with you. I have started a blog entitled www.siblinglossblog.com where we can share insights and struggles. Part of what I consider the gift of healing through and with others. I am thankful for all of us, for the amazing and enlightening books out there that I have enjoyed reading and consider a huge part of my spiritual journey.

Thank you so much for reading Sibling Loss.

NOTE

In closing, I must tell you about a fascinating incident that happened years ago while I was checking up on my parent's home, as I do every winter while they were in Florida. I was driven by some unknown source to a box that was hidden in the furthest corner of the least used closet in the house. Mathew's school books, as well as his personal effects which the police brought to us that dreadful night when they informed us of his accident, have been stored in that box for twenty-seven years. I shoved my hand into the middle of the box and took out one exercise book. Oddly enough, I opened it to the page that contained the last literary entry Mathew had made – a poem written either the day before or on the very day that he was killed.

I called Ottawa's archives and the Montreal School Board, who both confirmed that there was no record of any author having composed it. Although one can interpret the poem, which appears on the following page, simply as an expression of a boy's concern for a troubled planet it has confirmed my belief that Mathew was sent here on a sort of angelic mission. And if he's in that peaceful world he wrote about so long ago, I look forward to joining him there someday.

CLOSING POEM

FAR FAR AWAY

by Michael Ravinsky (the 60's)

Far, far away
Where the clouds are never gray,
I flew past my private rainbow
To the land that's bright and gay

Where the flowers always bloom,
And the stars are always bright,
Where the sun shines warm, and,
Then gives rise to a mystic, pleasant night

Children never cry here; nor,
do people ever sigh,
It's the land of youth and happiness,
of hello and not good-bye

For once you come to this land,
With no hate, or war, or strife,

You'd want to leave that world of ours,
And live there all your life.

But I'm afraid that just can't be,
For soon I lose its sight,
You see; the only time I visit
Is when, I'm fast asleep at night.

Made in the USA
Columbia, SC
02 February 2021

32096519R00105